START QUILTING

START QUILTING

All you need to know to start
making your own fabulous quilts

Celia Eddy

APPLE

A QUARTO BOOK

First published in the United Kingdom
by the Apple Press
Sheridan House, 112–116a Western Road
Hove, East Sussex BN3 1DD

ISBN 1-84092-337-6

QUAR.QUBA

Conceived, designed and produced by
Quarto Publishing plc
The Old Brewery
6 Blundell Street
London N7 9BH

Senior project editor **Nadia Naqib**
Art editor **Karla Jennings**
Designer **Elizabeth Healey**
Illustrators **Coral Mula, Jennie Dooge**
Text editors **Katherine James, Anne Plume**
Assistant art director **Penny Cobb**
Photographers **Ian Howes, Colin Bowling**
Indexer **Dorothy Frame**

Art director **Moira Clinch**
Publisher **Piers Spence**

Manufactured by Universal Graphics Pte Limited, Singapore
Printed by Star Standard Industries Pte Limited, Singapore

CONTENTS

INTRODUCTION

There are as many routes into quilting as there are quilters. Some of us are introduced to it by an enthusiastic friend, others fall in love with a quilt they come across and want to make something similar. Yet others may come across a book of quilts or patterns and feel inspired to 'give it a try'. Some people just get right down to work without worrying about 'right' and 'wrong' ways of doing things, which is exactly how I started. Of course, starting out like that has its downside: if I'd known then even half of what I do now, there wouldn't be a trunk in my spare bedroom filled with UFOs. (UFOs are UnFinished Objects, to be distinguished from WIPs, Works In Progress; when one becomes the other is a frequent topic of debate among quilters). Quilting tradition contains many, many 'dos and don'ts – some of them you'll find useful and some of them you'll discard. Only you can decide which things are right and wrong for you and if in the process of discovery you make mistakes, put them down as learning experiences and carry on!

However you begin, you'll realize your aims much more quickly and satisfyingly if you have some basic tools and guidelines – after that you can decide exactly how you want to work. For example, it's useful to know the different techniques needed for stitching by hand and by machine, after which you may decide that you're basically a hand stitcher or a machine stitcher – or, like me, use both methods from time to time.

Deciding what you need to buy to get started on quilting can be positively bewildering, especially if you visit a specialty supplier or store, where the range and quantity of things you are invited to buy is apparently unlimited. In the end, the choice of tools and equipment is personal, and one person's indispensable tool is another person's useless gadget. The Materials and Equipment section offers a selection of the tools and equipment which, after long trial and error, I'd recommend as the most useful in a basic quilting kit.

Equipment is one thing; knowing how to use it is something else! Again, there are usually at least two ways of achieving your desired result, but some basic 'how-tos' will help you to get good results right from the beginning. The Basic Skills section covers the building blocks for all the techniques and projects that follow, so it's worth spending a little time going through them before you begin. In the instructions for the projects, some of them are explained in more detail where necessary, and you may find you need to refer back to them when working through other projects.

Celia Eddy.

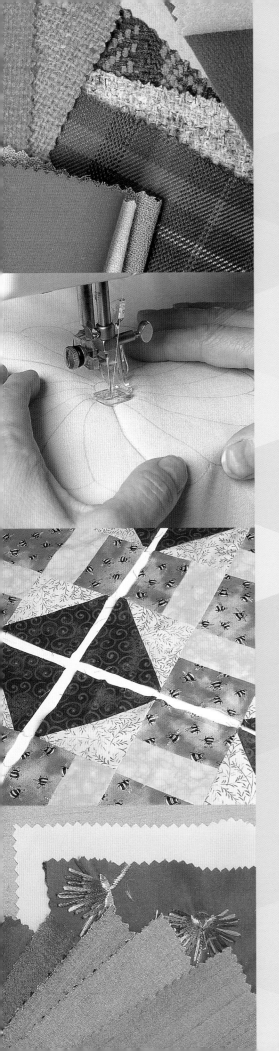

GETTING STARTED

The materials and equipment required for quilting are easily obtainable and relatively inexpensive. This section shows you the items that you will need to make a start in quilting. It also demonstrates all the fundamental quilting skills, such as making templates, joining blocks and adding borders that will help you stitch not just the projects in this book but many more patchwork and quilting designs, whether traditional or modern.

MATERIALS AND EQUIPMENT

When I started making patchwork, my equipment consisted of nothing more complicated than scissors, pins, needles, thimble, thread, fabric and some cardboard for templates. Those are the essentials for making patchwork. To quilt your patchwork, you need backing fabric, batting and quilting thread. It couldn't be simpler!

But, of course, things have moved on and today we have a wonderful selection of tools, equipment and special patchwork fabrics, all designed to make life easier and more fun for the quilter.

The following are the materials and tools that I find the most useful.

FOR DRAFTING AND DESIGN

Most art supply and craft shops stock the following:

- Graph paper for drawing full-size blocks
- Tracing paper
- Isometric paper, which is marked in triangles and is useful for drawing out hexagonal patterns, such as 'Tumbling Blocks' or 'Grandmother's Garden'
- Cardboard or mounting board (cereal boxes are fine!)
- Template plastic
- Lead pencils, hard and soft

- Good-quality coloured pencils
- Felt pens
- A pair of hinged mirrors – these are ideal for working out pattern repeats and kaleidoscope effects. They can be bought ready-made but you can easily make your own from two mirror-tiles joined with masking tape. Mirror tiles are available from DIY shops

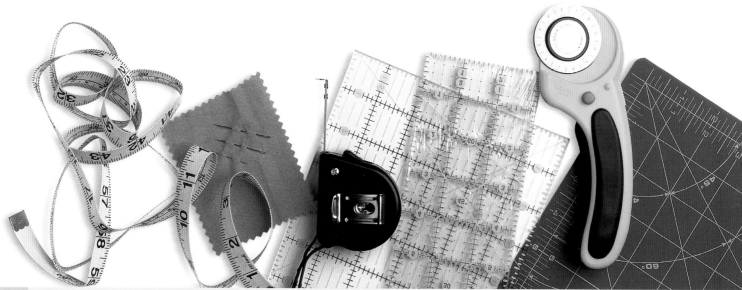

Computer Programs

If you're a computer user you can use some of the many available graphics programs to create quilt designs. There are also some excellent dedicated quilt programs that make quilt design easy and fun. With these, you can draft blocks yourself or use the blocks in the collections that the currently available quilting programs all contain. Blocks can be changed, resized and coloured, then set into quilts. You can design quilts and arrange sizes and layouts. Even the quantities of fabric required for any particular project can be calculated. Designing on the computer is great fun and the only problem you'll have is finding the time to make all the quilts you come up with!

Scissors

Scissors are a vital part of the quilter's toolkit and good-quality ones will give good results and last for years. You need:

① Large fabric scissors: spring-loaded handles are easy to use and especially useful for people with hand or wrist problems – and for people who want to avoid those problems

② Paper scissors, for cutting cardboard, paper and template plastic. Never use your fabric scissors for this purpose

③ Small sharp scissors for snipping machine threads, trimming corners and other small jobs. Always use these rather than your large fabric scissors to save the latter from becoming blunt

④ Rotary cutter and self-heal mat: for speedy cutting of lots of patches, these items are ideal. A useful average size of mat for general purposes is 43 x 58 cm (17 x 23 in). Cutters come in various sizes but the most useful has a 1¼ in. (3 cm) diameter blade.

⑤ Seam ripper: in a perfect world, we wouldn't make mistakes – but personally I find this little tool one of the most useful in my sewing kit. Use it for taking out stitches, removing basting stitches, or anything that needs a small, sharp point

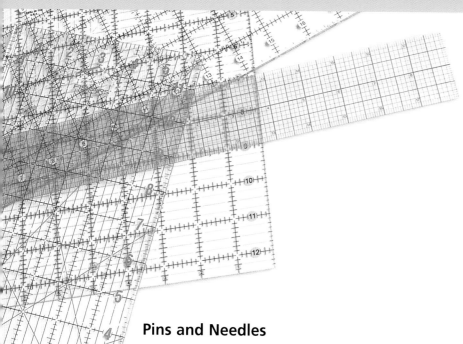

Rulers

You need rulers for drafting blocks and for measuring fabric. Here is a useful list of rulers:

- Acrylic ruler for use with rotary cutter and mat.
- Ruler at least 38 cm (15 in) long and 5 cm (2 in) wide, for drafting blocks.
- 30 cm (12 in) square for checking block dimensions.

Pins and Needles

Pins and needles are a vital part of the quilter's toolkit and good-quality ones will give good results and last for years. You need:

① Long, glass-headed pins for larger patches
② Flat-headed (or flower-headed) pins for pinning patches that are to be machine-sewn together, because the needle can run over them without damage
③ Ordinary (straight) dressmaker's pins
④ Extra long, fine glass-headed pins for pinning quilts together.
⑤ General-purpose needles in a variety of sizes for basting and for hand-sewing patches
⑥ Quilting needles for hand quilting, called 'betweens': these come in sizes from about 5 to 12, 12 being the smallest and finest; for most purposes, size 8 or 9 will be suitable

Tape Measures

As well as an ordinary dressmaker's tape measure, it is also useful to have a metal one for large quilts.

Thimbles

Many quilters like to use a thimble to avoid pricking their finger every time they take a stitch. There are two main types:

① Ordinary metal thimble for basic sewing

② Metal thimble with ridge around the crown for hand quilting

Threads

Try to buy good-quality threads – cheap threads may disintegrate in the seams and cause your patchwork to come apart, or may break or snag in the machine. You will need:

① Quilting threads for hand quilting

② Embroidery threads and metallic threads for embellishment

Hoops and Frames

In order to quilt, the three layers of the quilt have to be held taut in a frame or hoop so that they don't slip apart while you're sewing. The most useful are:

• Floor standing frames, either wooden or plastic, for large quilts

• Hoops for smaller items (illustrated below)

Markers

Traditionally, a variety of everyday household items were used for marking patterns on quilts prior to quilting. Here is a list of items that will come in handy:

① Quilter's silver pencil

② 2B pencils for marking fabric

③ Pigma pens for making permanent labels for the backs of quilts

④ Blue marker pen

Erasers

You will need erasers for removing pencil marks

⑤ Fabric eraser

⑥ Ordinary latex eraser

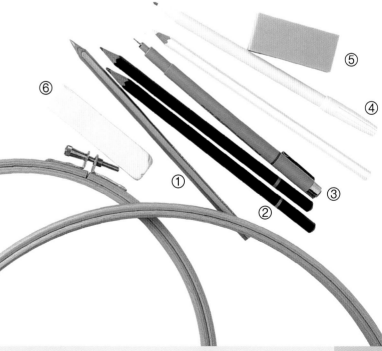

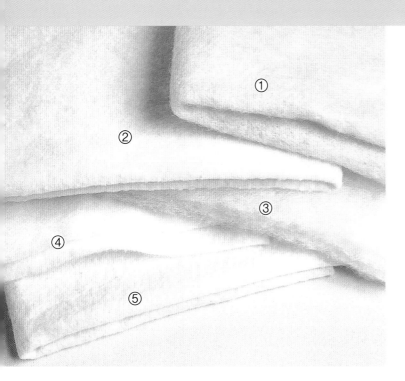

Batting

Batting is the inner lining between the top and bottom layers of a quilt and it is what gives a quilt its texture and bulk. Batting is manufactured from various fibres in a variety of thicknesses. These include:

① Wool

② Cotton

③ Good quality polyester, weight 112 g (4 oz). Quality is important because some cheaper versions will 'beard' – that is, the fibres will migrate through the quilt top and create a fuzzy effect on the surface; if in doubt, check with the retailer before purchasing

④ Good-quality polyester, weight 56 g (2 oz)

⑤ Needle-punched polyester

Templates and Template Kits

Templates and stencils are the master patterns for quilting. Sets or kits of heavy-duty plastic or acrylic templates are commercially available. You can also make your own templates by drawing the block in full size, cutting out each of the shapes necessary for the design, and gluing them onto cardboard or template plastic (see pages 16–17).

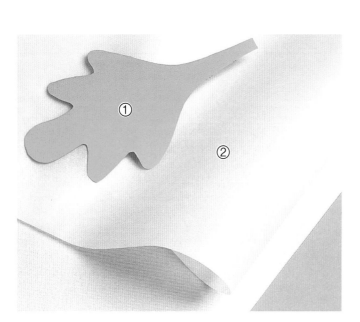

Appliqué

In the technique of appliqué, pieces of fabric are cut out and stitched onto a foundation. The main items you will need are:

① Thin cardboard

② Fusible webbing

Sewing Machine

Any machine that can produce straight, even stitching is adequate for making basic patchwork but modern electric and computerized machines provide many other useful features. The most useful of these are:

① Tension guide
② Stitch-width selector
③ Stitch pattern guide
④ Stitch length guide
⑤ Foot lever
⑥ Needle
⑦ Presser foot
⑧ Needle plate

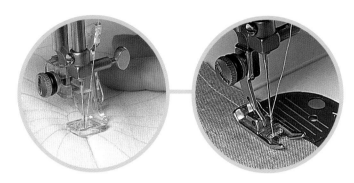

Darning foot   *General-purpose foot*

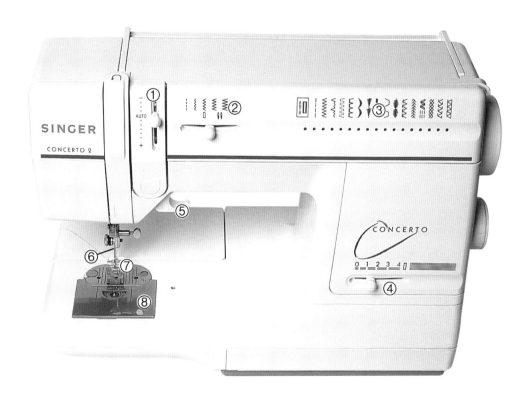

Fabrics

There is an endless variety of fabrics for the quilter to select from. The most suitable fabric for patchwork is 100 percent cotton. For backing or lining fabrics, you will need muslin or other pure cotton. For decorative items such as wall-quilts, bags and cushions, you can use satin, silk, velvet and brocade.

BASIC SKILLS

Commercial templates are available for most patchwork designs, but it's often more satisfying (and cheaper) to make your own.

BASIC SKILLS

WHAT YOU NEED
- Heavyweight paper, pencil, glue and marking pen
- Scissors, craft knife, rotary cutter and self-heal mat
- Fabrics – American patchwork cottons are best for beginners
- Fine sewing needle for hand sewing, or sewing machine
- Threads in colours to match fabrics
- Cardboard or template plastic

DRAFTING BLOCKS AND MAKING TEMPLATES

At its simplest, a quilt block is a unit made up of patches in different shapes and colours. A standard block is usually square – but it doesn't have to be. Blocks can be rectangular, hexagonal, or triangular. There is an almost infinite number of ways in which block patterns can be formed and they can be made by piecing (patchwork) or by appliqué. Lots of patchwork patterns can be purchased with ready-made templates, and you can also buy sets of templates in different shapes, all of which can be very convenient and timesaving. Sometimes, though, you may want to make a pattern for which you can't find a ready-made version, or even to make up one of your own, in which case it's useful to be able to draft blocks yourself and make your own templates

Many patchwork blocks can be drafted on grids, which makes drawing the templates easy. Here's how:

THE ANATOMY OF A QUILT

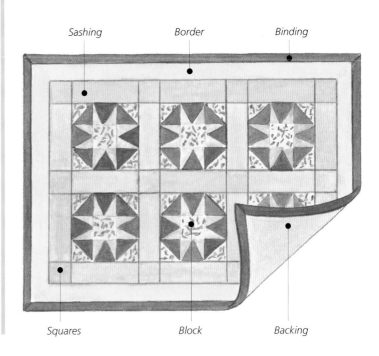

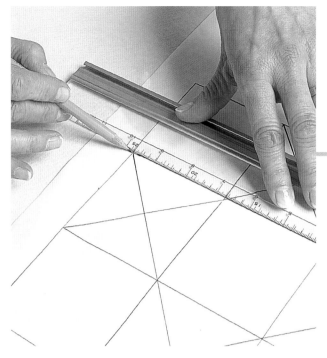

STEP 1
On heavyweight paper draw, in pencil, a square (or other shape) of the size you want your block to be, and draw a grid. Draw in the pattern of your block.

STEP 2
Go over the grid lines with a marking pen. Identify the shapes in the block and mark them A, B, C and so on. The illustration shows a simple nine-patch block, but the method can be applied to any block.

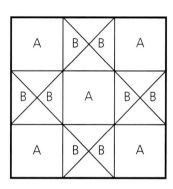

STEP 3
Cut out each piece using your paper scissors, and glue the paper shape onto cardboard or template plastic. Add a seam allowance: using a ruler and a sharp pencil or marking pen, draw a line exactly 0.625 cm (¼ in) around the whole shape. Cut out on the seam allowance line using sharp scissors or a craft knife.

Seam Allowance
The seam allowance is the area of fabric between the stitching line and the cut edge. The seam allowance allows room for handling and adjusting size. It is important to keep the stitching lines accurate, so that the block does not become too large or too small.

TIP

You'll find it useful to make a quick sketch of your block and to colour it in to indicate where the different colours and fabrics will go.

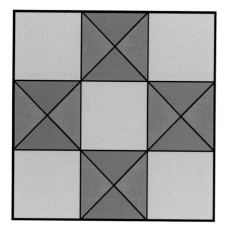

CUTTING PATCHES

The most important thing to remember when you are cutting your fabric is accuracy. If the patches aren't cut accurately, they won't fit together properly.

STEP 1 Note how many shapes and patches you need of each of the different fabrics you've chosen. Press these fabrics. Lay each template on the fabric and draw around it using a soft (2B) pencil.

STEP 2 Cut out exactly on the line using sharp fabric scissors.

TIME-SAVER

When pressing the fabric, use spray starch to stabilize it, to give it a nice crisp finish and to make the cutting process easier and more accurate.

Using a Rotary Cutter and Mat

If you're working on a large project, say a quilt with several repeated blocks, a rotary cutter and self-heal mat will make things a lot quicker and easier. But beware: the blade of the cutter is extremely sharp, so it's important to follow some simple safety rules when using this equipment:

- At the end of each cut, always put on the lock, which all cutters have. If possible, buy a cutter with an automatic lock, which retracts the blade as soon as you stop cutting.
- Always run the blade away from you, never towards you.
- Always keep the cutter in a safe place, well away from children.

STEP 1 Press the fabric really well – see the Time-saver tip opposite on using starch. You can cut several layers at a time if you make sure that the fabric is well pressed, especially the folds. Trim the fabric on your right. (Note: these instructions assume that you're right-handed – reverse them if you are left-handed.) Place your left hand firmly on the ruler and push the blade smoothly along the edge.

STEP 2 Turn the trimmed edge to your left, lay the ruler along the trimmed edge in line with the measurement you need, and cut along the edge of the ruler.

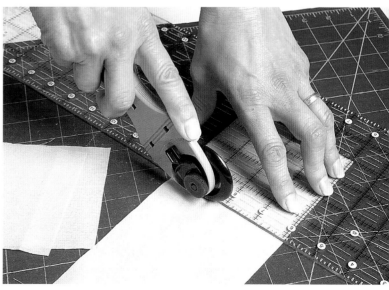

STEP 3 To make patches from the strips, line up as before with the markings on the ruler. Make triangles by cutting across the squares.

Basic Hand Stitching

Nothing could be simpler than sewing patchwork! It needs only a straightforward running stitch, except for English patchwork, where patches are joined by whipstitching them together.

Use a fine, sharp needle and thread to match your fabric. Begin and end each seam exactly 0.5 cm (¼ in) before the end – that is, do not sew into the seam allowance. You may find it helpful at first to draw in the stitching line as a guide, marking a small dot where stitching begins and ends. Take a small backstitch at the beginning and end of each seam and work with even-spaced running stitches along the seam allowance.

Hand-stitch English patchwork by placing the basted patches right sides together and neatly whipstitching the edges together. Start at the edge of the patches and sew to the end, anchoring the stitches with small backstitches at each end.

For appliqué it is best to use either a small hemming stitch or blanket stitch.

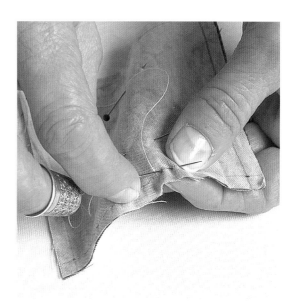

TIME-SAVER

When making lots of blocks, you can speed things up by using 'chain-piecing' to sew patches together. Line up the patches and feed them under the needle continuously, taking several stitches between patches.

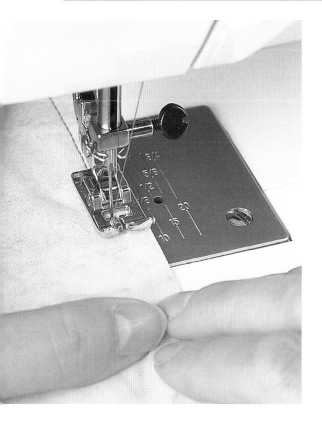

Basic Machine Stitching

A straight running stitch is all that's required to join patches and blocks by machine. Check that the tension on your machine is even and set the stitch length to between 9 and 12 stitches to the inch (2.5 cm). Lay the patches right sides together so that edges are even. Stitch exactly 0.5 cm (¼ in) along the edge.

The seam allowance is important because if it is uneven the units of the block won't meet up neatly, and your blocks may all end up different sizes (see page 17). Here are two good ways to get an accurate seam allowance:

Use a special 0.5 cm (¼ in) foot, if your machine has one.

Mark the throat plate of your machine so that you can see where to sew. Place a ruler under the machine needle and lower the needle so that it rests exactly on the 0.5 cm (¼ in) mark. With the ruler still in position, run a strip of marking tape alongside it. Place the edge of the fabric against the tape.

Setting in Patches

Some blocks include patches with awkward angles. These can only be pieced by setting the patches into the angles, which sounds complicated but is easy when you know how. Learning this method means that you'll be able to tackle many beautiful blocks that can only be pieced like this.

Setting in patches is easy as long as you remember not to sew into the seam allowance. You'll find it best to mark the end of the sewing line with a small dot.

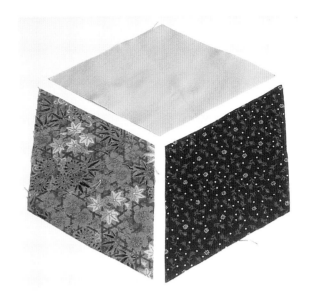

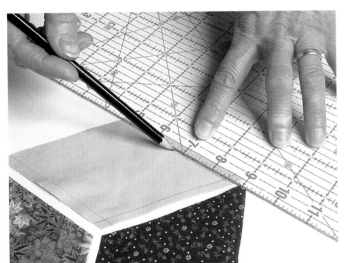

STEP 1 Lay out the patches in the arrangement in which they will be sewn.

STEP 2 On the back of each patch, mark the sewing lines, ie. 0.5 cm (¼ in) from the edge. Mark the end of each line with a small dot.

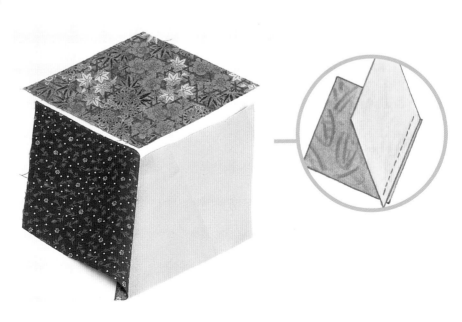

STEP 3 Place the first two patches right sides together and sew the seam between the marked dots. At the beginning and end, anchor the thread with a small backstitch.

STEP 4
Place the third patch on one patch and sew them together, sewing only up to the marked dot.

STEP 5
Gently press the completed block, first from the back and then on the front.

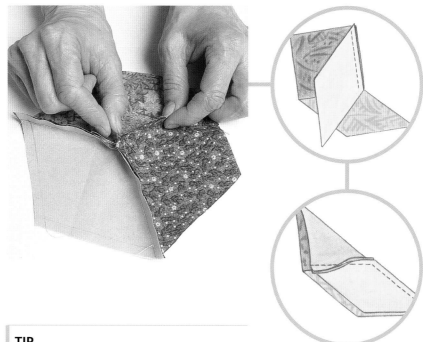

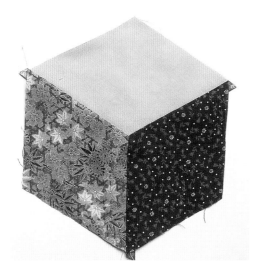

TIP

Although cotton patchwork fabrics today are usually fast to light and water, it's still worth pre-washing the dark fabrics to check that they won't bleed.

SETTINGS AND LAYOUTS

When all your blocks are made, you have several choices about how to assemble them into a quilt. The easiest thing is simply to join them in straight rows, but setting them diagonally, or 'on point', creates an interesting effect, or you might want to add borders or sashings (strips between the blocks).

Lay your blocks out on a large flat surface (a bed is ideal) and try out various settings and arrangements, plus colours and fabrics for borders and sashings. When you're happy with your choices, arrange all the blocks in position, or make a quick sketch to remind you of the order of assembly as you work.

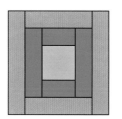

Sashings are vertical or horizontal strips between the single blocks (left) of a quilt, which create a lattice effect (below). (See page 41).

WORKING WITH COLOUR

We all have our personal favourite colours, and those that we hate and decide never to use, so laying down hard and fast rules for colour choice is difficult. Of course, the most important consideration in choosing colours is what pleases you and is appropriate to the quilt you want to make, but some general guidelines are useful in selecting fabrics, especially when you're planning a large project and don't want to find later that you've made a mistake on a grand scale.

First, spend a little time looking at how colours work together. Look at a colour wheel (right) and notice how the three so-called primary colours (red, blue and yellow) grade into each other, moving through all the shades between them. Colours which are opposite each

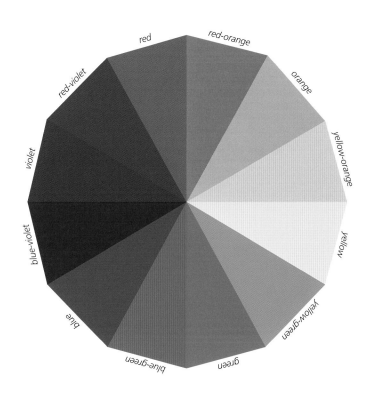

This colour wheel shows primary, secondary and tertiary colours. The primary colours are red, yellow and blue. The secondary colours are made by mixing two primary colours together, producing orange, green or violet. A tertiary colour is produced by mixing a primary colour with the secondary colour nearest to it on the wheel. The tertiary colours here are red-orange, yellow-orange, yellow-green, blue-green, blue-violet and red-violet.

Complementary colours

Colour hues

Colour value

Colour intensity

other on the colour wheel are said to be 'complementary colours', for example red and green or orange and blue. A useful aid when choosing colours is the collection of paint colour cards that you can get from a DIY shop. With this you can try different colours against each other before moving on to mixing and matching different fabrics. It's also useful to recognize some basic colour terms:

Hue is simply the name of a colour red, violet or green, for example.

Value is a term used to describe the lightness or darkness of the colour, that is, its position on a scale from white to black.

Intensity describes the brightness, depth and impact of the colour.

All colours are described by temperature: some are in the 'warm' range – reds and purples – others in the 'cool' range – blues and greens. The colour wheel shows you where the different ranges merge into each other. This knowledge can help you to set the mood or style for a quilt; for example, a quilt with a winter theme might include a variety of blue and white fabrics, whereas a quilt celebrating summer might contain a range of red, yellow and orange fabrics. In patchwork as well as colour it's important to use contrast between light and dark to highlight the pattern, remembering that dark colours tend to advance to the eye and light ones to retreat.

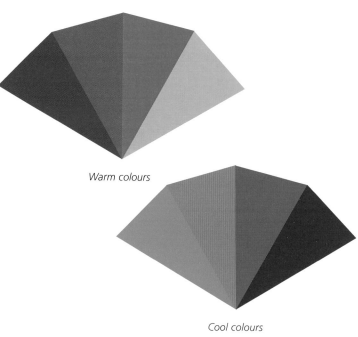

Warm colours

Cool colours

Some colours appear to advance, while others seem to recede. If you want to make something seem to come towards the viewer, warm colours such as reds and oranges are the best ones to choose. Blues and greens seem to recede when set next to a red.

The perception of colours can be affected by the colour context in which they're placed. For example, if you put a yellow border round a scrap quilt comprising many colours, the yellows in the quilt will stand out. If you add a blue border, the blues will appear dominant.

An easy but effective way to achieve a coherent look to your quilt, particularly if you're a beginner, is to choose from one of the many ranges of co-ordinated fabric that most manufacturers of patchwork cottons produce. These may include plains, large and small prints, checks and stripes, and are a wonderful aid to successful colour choice. You can always supplement the range by adding your own fabric choices.

When you're ready to work on your project, draw an outline of the pattern on cardboard, snip small pieces of the selected fabrics and place them on the drawing. When you're happy with the way the colours work together you can lightly glue them to the cardboard and keep it for reference as you work.

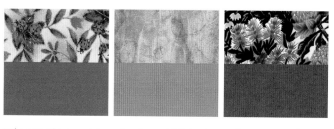

When combining plain and patterned fabrics in a quilt, try to match the colour of the plain fabric to a dominant colour in the pattern.

TIP

It's a great asset to be able to view fabrics and patterns at a distance and on a flat surface – ideally a wall. If you don't have space for a dedicated design wall, don't worry, improvise! Hang or pin a sheet on a door or wall, and pin fabrics and patterns to that.

Working with Fabrics

How will your finished item be used? As a special quilt to be kept for 'best'? As a quilt for a son or daughter going to university? As a serviceable bag? As a decorative wall quilt?

For washable bed-quilts choose 100 percent cotton fabrics that will stand repeated washing without the fabrics bleeding or shrinking.

For items such as bags that will get repeated hard wear, use strong cotton such as upholstery fabrics or thick calico, which are designed to take lots of wear and tear.

If you're making a decorative wall-panel that won't go in the wash you can be a bit more adventurous and incorporate more delicate fabrics, such as silk, satin or velvet.

TIP

A plain cream or black fabric, used as the main background colour of a quilt top, provides a strong contrast to most colour schemes. If you want to create a softer effect, use white or grey fabrics that have a motif on them in the same subtle shades of neutral colour.

TECHNIQUES & PROJECTS

This section takes you step-by-step through several traditonal quilting techniques, such as English Patchwork and Log Cabin Patchwork. It also looks at techniques of hand and machine appliqué as well as ways in which you can use a quilting hoop. Each technique is followed by a project that shows you how you can apply the technique in practice to make something of value for your friends or family.

One of the joys of quilting is the potential for real creativity once you've mastered the most important techniques. The possibilities are endless, and this section will hopefully launch you on your way to making and designing many more beautiful quilts.

AMERICAN BLOCK PATCHWORK

Making quilts in blocks was certainly a method known and used in Europe, but it was when it reached America with the early settlers that it flowered as a uniquely American form of folk art. The sewing together of patches by placing them right sides together and joining them with small running stitches is now universally known as 'American' patchwork, as distinct from 'English' patchwork, which is worked over paper templates with the patches whipstitched together (see page 20).

One reason for the development of the block system of working was almost certainly purely practical: blocks are easily portable and can be picked up and worked on at odd moments – no doubt very necessary when families were often on the move or there was limited space in which to work. Only when all the blocks for a quilt were completed was it necessary to find space to assemble something as large as a quilt.

Squares for Blocks

At its simplest, a block is a unit made up of patches in different shapes and colours that form the pattern (see page 16). Most American patchwork blocks are square because that is the easiest shape to fit together. It also makes it easy to work out how many blocks you will need for the size of the quilt you are going to make. Many blocks have been given names based either on the pattern itself or perhaps on the maker. Others are named to commemorate famous people, places or events. You could say that the whole of American history is reflected in the names of quilt blocks!

MAKING AMERICAN BLOCK PATCHWORK

WHAT YOU NEED

- Templates, or strong cardboard or plastic to make your own, as described in Basic Skills
- Scissors, or a rotary cutter and self-heal mat
- Fabrics – American patchwork cottons are best for beginners
- Fine sewing needle for hand sewing or sewing machine
- Threads in colours to match those of your patchwork or neutral threads if you're using several different colours

TIP

The standard size for patchwork blocks is 30 cm (12 in) finished. This makes it easy to work out the number of blocks you will need to make for a bed-sized quilt.

MAKING A SINGLE BLOCK

First make templates for your chosen block as shown in Basic Skills (pages 16–17) – or use ready-made templates, but make sure they include a 0.5 cm (¼ in) seam allowance. Next, cut out patches in selected shapes and colours.

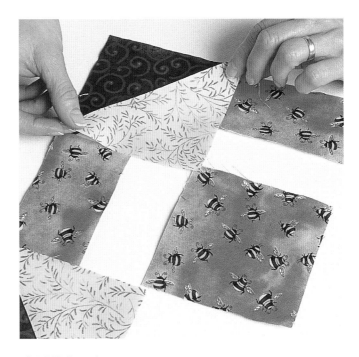

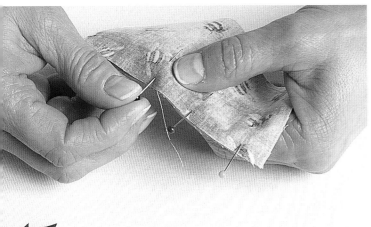

STEP 1 Lay out the patches as they appear in the block. Always try to arrange them so that they can be joined in straight rows, but if some of the shapes need set-in seams, follow the Basic Skills instructions for doing this.

STEP 2 Join patches by placing two right sides together, pinning them together and stitching exactly 0.5 cm (¼ in).(0.5 cm) from the edge.

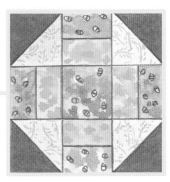

STEP 3 When you have sewn any two patches together, join a unit of two patches to the next and so on as described in Step 2.

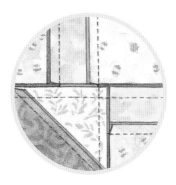

STEP 4 Join the rows. Finger-press joining seams in opposite directions before pinning, which will make it easier to match joining seams.

STEP 5 Press the completed block carefully from the back, taking care not to stretch the fabrics. Press down and then lift the iron to reposition it, rather than pushing it over the surface.

STEP 6 Turn to the front and then press again.

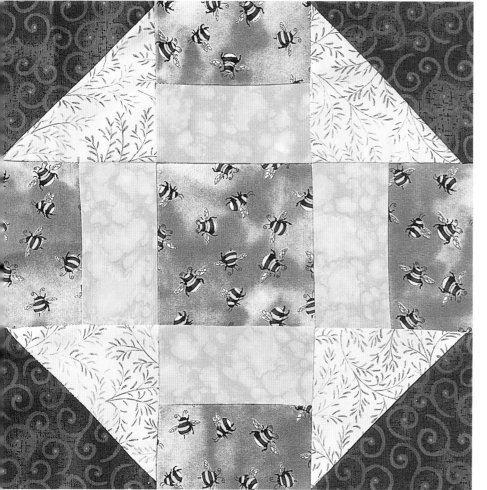

TIME-SAVER

As each block is completed, check that its measurements are accurate by using a 30 cm (12 in) square. It's much easier to correct any errors at this stage than when you are putting the blocks together.

Assembling Blocks to Make a Quilt

ASSEMBLING BLOCKS

What You Need
- Backing fabric
- Batting
- Pins
- Needle and basting thread
- Tape measure

STEP 1 Lay out the blocks in the setting of your choice, then pin and join in rows, using 0.5 (¼ in) seam allowance.

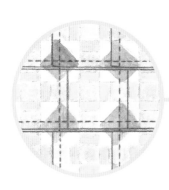

STEP 2 Join the rows, still using 0.5 cm (¼ in) seam allowance. Where the seams meet, press them to opposite sides to reduce bulk. Complete the quilt by adding borders or binding.

Attaching Borders

STEP 1 Decide on the width of borders, for example 7.5 cm (3 in). Measure the quilt top from side to side and cut two border strips of this length. Pin in position and sew to the top and bottom edges. Press the border strips open.

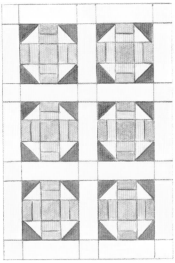

STEP 2 Measure
again, from top to bottom
including the added
borders and cut two
border strips of this length.
Pin and attach to the sides
of the quilt top. Press the
border strips open.

MITERING BORDERS

If you prefer, you can join the corners of the border with a
diagonal seam, known as 'mitering'. To do this:

STEP 1 Measure the length and
width of the quilt top, plus seam allowances.
Cut border strips of these measurements, but
then add twice the width of the border to the
length of each strip. Pin the borders to the
quilt top on all four sides, right sides together,
leaving equal extensions at both ends.

STEP 2 Lay out the patchwork flat and let the
extensions overlap each other.

TIP

Always measure through the middle of the quilt, as any distortions
or inaccuracies will show up on the edges. It's much better to cut
the borders to the centre measurements and ease them into position.
That way, your quilt should be square and even, measuring the
same on all sides.

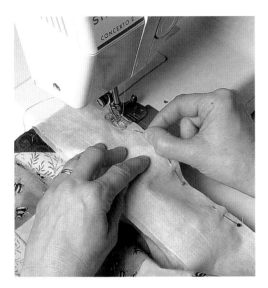

STEP 3
Stitch the borders on all sides but do not stitch into the seam allowances at the end of each strip. Backstitch in order to secure at the end of each border.

STEP 4
Press the borders open.

STEP 5
Turn the top layer under at an angle of 45 degrees.

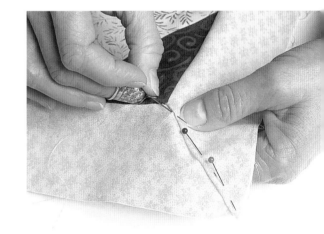

STEP 6
Pin the top layer as shown and slipstitch it into place.

STEP 7
Trim off the excess fabric from behind. Turn to the front of the work and press the seam.

ASSEMBLING A QUILT

Once your pieced top is complete, the next stage is to turn it into a quilt.

ASSEMBLING A QUILT

WHAT YOU NEED
- Backing or lining fabric – fine muslin or other cotton
- Batting
- Long glass-headed pins
- Basting thread
- Long needle

STEP 1 Measure the quilt and cut backing and batting a good 1.25 cm (½ in) larger all around. Lay out the backing fabric right side down. Lay batting on top of it. Finally, place patchwork right side up on the batting. Pin the three layers together using long glass-headed pins.

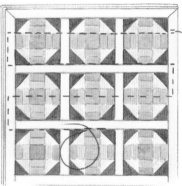

STEP 2 Baste the entire quilt surface using a large needle and placing stitches evenly. First baste across the quilt, and then up and down it.

FINISHING A QUILT

The quilt can be finished either by tying or by quilting – you'll find instructions for tying in the project on page 38, and different methods of quilting in later projects. When quilting is complete, all that remains is to finish the edges of the quilt. There are several methods to choose from.

Binding

STEP 1 Trim the edges of the backing and batting even with the quilt top.

STEP 2
Cut 6 cm (2½ in) wide strips of the binding fabric on the straight grain. Fold the strips in half lengthwise, wrong sides together.

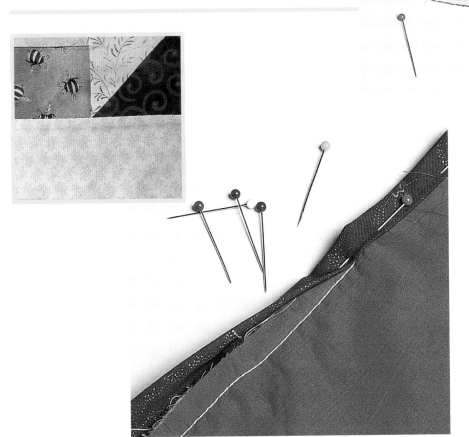

STEP 3
Pin the strips to the top and bottom of the quilt with the raw edges of the binding strips running along the raw edge of the quilt, and stitch through all the layers.

STEP 4
Trim back the batting close to the seam to reduce bulk, and fold the binding to the back. Pin, then slipstitch the binding onto the backing. Repeat the process for the sides, taking care to fold the edges under at the corners.

Self-binding

In this method the edge of the quilt is enclosed by bringing the backing fabric over to the front, turning it under and hemming it down. Of course, you can only use this method if you've left enough extra backing fabric to fold over to the right side of the quilt top.

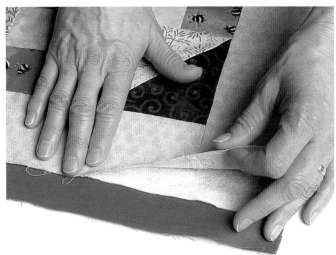

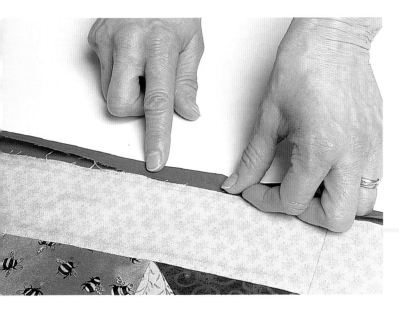

STEP 1 Trim the quilt top and batting so that they are even.

STEP 2 Fold the backing so that its raw edge meets the edge of the quilt top. Press.

STEP 3 Turn the folded backing onto the front of the quilt and pin.

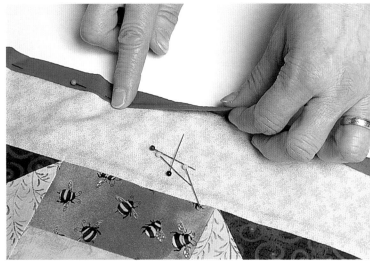

STEP 4 Finish by hemming the overlapped edge to the quilt top.

Butted Edge

This is a very economical method of finishing as it needs no extra fabric.

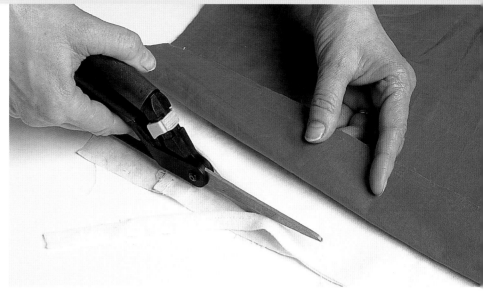

STEP 1 Trim all three layers of the backing, batting and quilt top so that they are even. Then trim the batting by about 1.25 cm (½ in) from the quilt top.

STEP 2 Fold the quilt top over the batting. Pin and baste through all three layers.

STEP 3 Fold the backing over the batting and quilt top. The quilt top should slightly overlap the backing, which should not show on the quilt top. Pin, baste and neatly slipstitch the layers together.

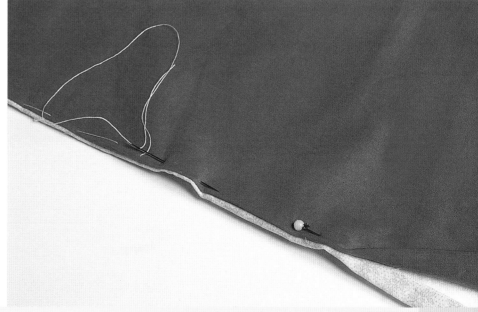

TIP

One advantage of using binding fabric (instead of the backing or quilt top) to finish a quilt is that you can replace the binding if it gets frayed.

PROJECT 1:
STAR OF THE WEST

Finished size: 76 x 76 cm (30 x 30 in)

This quick and easy wall decoration will enhance your home and can be made in colours to suit any décor. The Star of the West block used is a traditional one, sometimes also known as Clay's Choice. Four repeated star blocks couldn't be easier to piece but produce a pleasing effect when they are joined. The quilt is finished with plain borders, then assembled, tied and the edges bound.

WHAT YOU NEED

- Fabric 1: 0.35 m (⅜ yard) floral
- Fabric 2: 0.35 m (⅜ yard) lilac
- Fabric 3: (0.45 m (½ yard) yellow
- Farbic 4: 0.8 m (⅞ yard) (for borders and binding)
- Backing fabric
- Batting 81 x 81 cm (32 x 32 in)
- Perle cotton or embroidery floss for tying

TEMPLATES A AND B

Follow the instructions on pages 16–17 for making templates A and B. Decide on fabric placement.

Cut patches as follows:

Fabric 1: 16 from template A;
           16 from template B

Fabric 2: 16 from template A;
           16 from template B

Fabric 3: 32 from template B

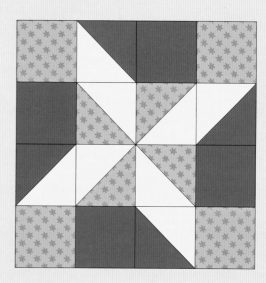

INSTRUCTIONS

STEP 1 Piece four blocks
as shown. Press each block as it is completed, and check the measurements. Correct any inaccuracies at this stage.

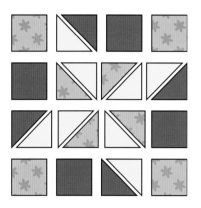

STEP 2 Pin the blocks
together in pairs, matching the seams carefully. Join the two pairs.

Measure the quilt top from side to side through the center. It should measure 62 cm (24½ in).

STEP 3 Cut two 9 cm
(3½ in) strips of border fabric of this length, and join to the top and bottom of the quilt.

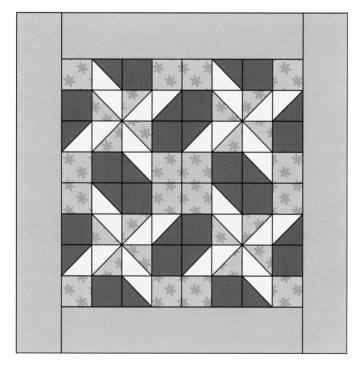

STEP 4 Measure the quilt from
top to bottom, including the newly added borders, and cut two (9 cm) 3½ in) strips of this length. Join to the sides of the quilt. Press the whole top but take care not to stretch the patchwork.

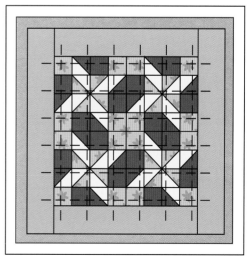

STEP 5 Lay out the backing fabric right side
down on a flat surface. Place the batting on top of it. Then lay the quilt top on the batting right side up. Pin all three layers then baste.

STEP 6
Using a long needle and either perle cotton or embroidery floss, begin tying the quilt working from the centre. Place ties at all the corners where the patches meet. Push the needle straight down through the three layers, leaving a tail of about 5 cm (2 in) on the surface. Bring the needle up a small distance from the point at which the needle entered. Holding on to the 'tail', take another small stitch and cut off the thread so that you have two 'tails' on the surface. Tie them with a double knot and trim off evenly.

TIP

When joining border strips to make a strip long enough for your quilt, you will make the joins less obvious if you cut and join the fabric on a slant, at an angle of 45 degrees.

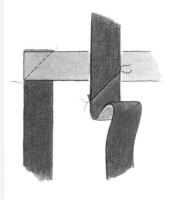

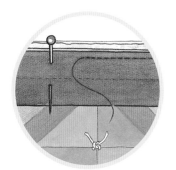

STEP 7
Trim the backing and batting exactly even with the quilt top. Measure the width and length of your quilt and cut four 6 cm (2½ in) strips of fabric 2, adding 2.5 cm (1 in) extra to the length for turnings at each end of the binding. Fold strips in half wrong sides together and press well. Pin the first strip to the edge of the right side of the quilt with raw edges together. Stitch through all the layers. Repeat for the opposite side of the quilt. Turn the strips to the back and hem or slipstitch to the backing fabric. Repeat for the other two sides, but leave enough to turn under at the ends.

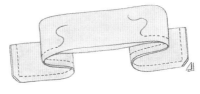

STEP 8
Add a 7.5 (3 in) wide hanging sleeve. Cut 16.5 cm (6½ in) wide strips of backing fabric or plain muslin, 2.5 cm (1 in) less than the width of the quilt. Fold in half and seam the raw edges together, leaving a small gap in the seam. Turn inside out through the gap, press out the corners with sharp scissors, and press the seam. Close the opening by slipstitching. Pin the sleeve to the back of the quilt just below the binding. Slipstitch into position.

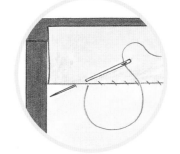

STEP 9
The finishing touch: don't forget to add a label to your quilt with your name, the date and perhaps a dedication if it's intended as a gift. Remember – today's quilts are tomorrow's heirlooms!

Quilt Layout

Making Sashings

What You Need
- Fabrics for sashings and squares (if any)
- Scissors, or a rotary cutter and self-heal mat
- Pins, to hold the sashings together for stitching
- Fine sewing needle for hand sewing
- Threads in colours to match fabrics

When all the blocks for your quilt are pieced, decide how they will look best in the quilt. You can simply join the blocks in straight rows, set them diagonally (known as 'on point'), or set alternate pieced or appliquéd blocks with plain blocks.

One way to enhance the effect is to add strips between the blocks, called 'sashings'. Sashings also add to the size of the quilt so you must add them, plus any borders, to the final dimensions when working out backing and batting.

Setting Blocks with Sashings

Sashings are vertical and horizontal strips between the blocks. They create a grid, or lattice effect and can either be plain or have squares in contrasting fabric where the strips meet. To add sashings, you need extra fabric that complements the blocks in the quilt top.

It is important to add 0.5 cm (¼ in) seam allowance to all your measurements when cutting strips.

Decide on the width of the sashing, which should be in proportion to the size of the blocks. A 7.5 cm (3 in) wide sashing looks in scale with a standard block. Each row of blocks is joined by strips the same length as the blocks, for example 30 cm (12 in) for 30 cm (12 in) blocks. (Note: the unfinished blocks will measure 32 cm (12½ in), so that's the length to cut the sashing strips.)

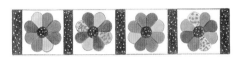

STEP 1 Count the number of joining strips needed. For example, to join four blocks you need three strips plus one each for the beginning and end of the row. Work out how many sashing strips you need and cut that number.

STEP 2 Place a sashing strip right sides together on the first block, pin and stitch.

STEP 3 Place the next sashing strip on the other side of the block, pin and stitch. Press all seams the same way, away from the sashing. Continue in this way until the row of blocks is joined.

STEP 4

Work out how many long sashing strips will be needed, depending on how many rows of blocks there are. Measure the rows and cut strips of this length. Two extra strips will be needed, one for the top and one for the bottom.

Sashings With Squares

You might like to highlight sashings by adding squares at the points where the sashing strips meet. Count the number of joining strips needed, including strips for the top and bottom of the quilt as for plain sashings. Join the blocks in rows with sashings strips, adding one at each end of the row as above.

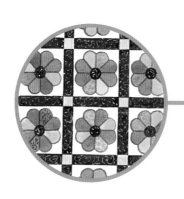

STEP 1

Cut squares exactly the same size as the width of the sashing strips.

STEP 2

Make horizontal strips by joining squares and sashing strips, beginning and ending each row with a square. Join rows of blocks with strips, taking care to match the seams where the sashings meet. Finally, add a row of sashing strips and squares to the top and one to the bottom.

Easy Machine Stitching 'In the Ditch'

This is a quick and easy method for anchoring patchwork to backing and batting. It's ideal when you want a quilted effect without the quilting stitches showing.

Successful machine quilting depends on preparing both your quilt and your machine properly. Make sure that the machine is properly oiled, and check that there is no build-up of lint around the bobbin case. (Your seam ripper will come in handy for removing any unwanted deposits). Set the tension on your sewing machine a little slacker than for ordinary sewing and use a slightly longer stitch. If possible, use a walking foot, also known as an 'even-feed' foot. You'll find more detailed instructions on machine quilting in Log Cabin Patchwork, page 72. If possible, use invisible thread (monofilament) in the top spool and ordinary machine thread in the bobbin – that way any wobbles in the line of stitching won't show up.

TIME-SAVER

To keep a firm grip on the quilt top while stitching, it helps if you wear a pair of cotton gloves – gardening gloves with small rubber dots on the palms are ideal.

STEP 1 Assemble and baste the quilt as explained in American Block Patchwork, page 28. Position the quilt under the sewing machine. If it's a large quilt, roll it up from the right-hand side. Place the hands firmly on the quilt on either side of the needle to guide it along the seam lines.

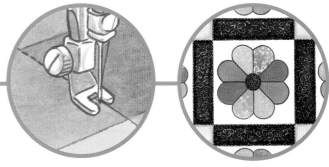

STEP 2 Stitch between the blocks exactly on top of the seam lines. When quilting is complete, use a needle or seam ripper to draw both threads to the back of the quilt, tie the ends and snip off.

PROJECT 2:
BABY'S PLAY MAT

Finished size: 48 x 48 in. (122 x 122 cm)

Nine easy-to-piece blocks are set with sashings and borders. This well-padded quilt in bright, cheerful colours makes an ideal play area for baby – just right for a Christmas or birthday present. Of course, the quilt can also be used as a warm lap-quilt or as a wall-hanging. When choosing fabrics for this project, remember that it will get hard wear and frequent washing so be sure to choose sturdy, washable fabrics. The original quilt for this project was made from flannel fabrics that combine the advantages of washing and wearing well and softness.

WHAT YOU NEED

- 0.25 m (¼ yard) each of at least six different fabrics for the strips from which the blocks are constructed
- 0.25 m (¼ yard) of fabric for the center squares
- 1 m (1 yard) of fabric for the borders
- Backing fabric 124 x 124 cm (49 x 49 in)
- Thick-quality batting 124 x 124 cm (49 x 49 in)

INSTRUCTIONS

In each block two different fabrics are used to surround the centre square. You can vary the fabrics in the blocks as much as you like, but each round in the block should be of the same fabric. All the strips are cut 6 cm (2½ in) wide.

STEP 1 Cut nine 11 cm (4½ in) squares for the centers of the nine blocks.

First round–Fabric 1 Cut two strips 11 cm (4½ in) long. Join to opposite sides of the center square, right sides together. Open out and press.

Cut two strips 21 cm (8½ in) long. Join to opposite sides of the centre square.

Second round–Fabric 2 Cut two strips 21 cm (8½ in) long. Join to opposite sides of the block.

Cut two strips 31 cm (12½ in) long and join to opposite sides to complete the block. Make eight more blocks like this.

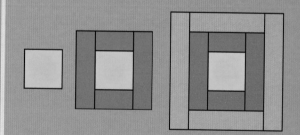

STEP 2

Sashings and borders Cut 9 x 31 cm (3½ x 12½ in) strips from sashing fabric. Cut six of these. Join the first row of three blocks with sashing strips, placing the strips on the blocks right sides together. Join the second and third rows in the same way.

TIP

To measure the size of your blocks, remember to measure them from seam line to seam line and not from the raw edges of the blocks.

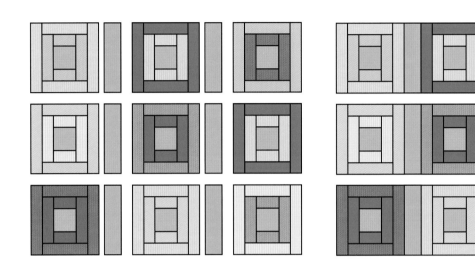

STEP 3

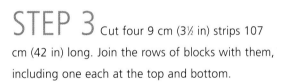

Cut four 9 cm (3½ in) strips 107 cm (42 in) long. Join the rows of blocks with them, including one each at the top and bottom.

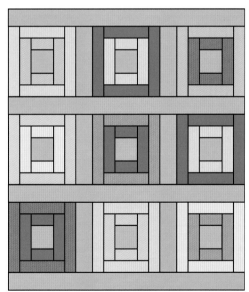

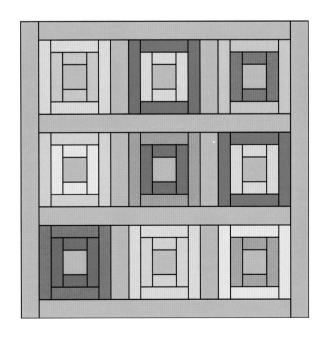

STEP 4

Cut two strips 123 cm (48½ in) long and attach to the sides of the quilt top.

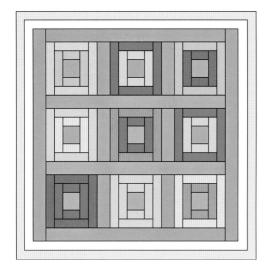

STEP 5 **Assembling** Lay out the backing fabric right side down, then the batting on top of it. Lay the pieced patchwork on top, right side up.

STEP 6 Pin with long glass pins or flower pins and then baste all over, first horizontally and then vertically.

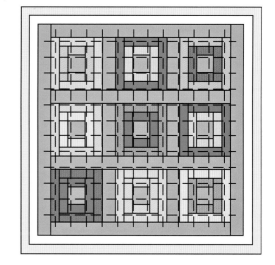

STEP 7 **Quilting** The quilt is finished by an easy method known as 'stitching in the ditch', (see page 43). Ideally you should use a walking (or even-feed) foot if you have one. To ensure that the stitching is really invisible, you can use monofilament thread in the top spool and ordinary thread in the bobbin.

Place the basted quilt top under the needle, if necessary rolling one side up so that you can work on one section at a time. Quilt through all layers along the seam lines. At the end of each line, take a backstitch to secure the stitches.

TIME-SAVER

You can use bulldog clips or bicycle clips to secure the rolled-up section. When you're ready for the next section, unroll and re-clip.

TIME-SAVER

If you can't find the thicker batting needed for this project, try using two layers of an ordinary batting.

STEP 8 **Finishing the edges** Use the 'butted edge' method (page 37) to finish the edges. This is a very economical way of finishing the edges as it doesn't use any extra fabric. Slipstitch the edges together as neatly as possible.

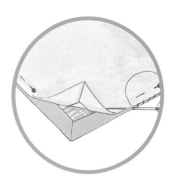

ENGLISH PATCHWORK

The method of making patchwork over paper templates is also known as English patchwork. The patches, which are made by basting fabric over the templates, are then hand stitched together with small stitches taken across the tops of the patches.

The Advantages of English Patchwork

There are several advantages to this method of patchwork. For one thing, it makes it easier to handle difficult fabrics, such as silk and satin, because the papers anchor them while they are being sewn together. Also, it's a very portable type of work, which can be picked up and worked on in odd moments. Perhaps best of all, it makes working awkward angles easy, which is one reason it's often called 'mosaic' patchwork – complicated geometrical shapes can easily be fitted together just as in mosaic tiles.

Although the making of patchwork almost certainly has its early roots in the recycling of fabrics, by the early Victorian period this style of working had become popular as a hobby even among women who had no need at all to economize, and there are plenty of surviving examples from the period.

Apart from the advantages mentioned above, perhaps most persuasively of all, in a busy world hand sewing is relaxing and therapeutic. You may not want to embark on a large bed quilt with this method, but it's perfect for smaller projects such as cushions, bags, baby quilts and table covers.

HOW TO MAKE ENGLISH PATCHWORK

WHAT YOU NEED

- Strong cardboard or template plastic to make a master template or a commercially made acrylic or metal template
- Medium-weight paper for paper templates
- Paper scissors
- Fabric scissors (never use your sharp fabric scissors for cutting anything else)
- Fine sewing needle
- Thread
- Small pieces of fabric

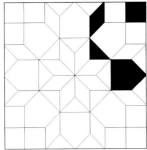

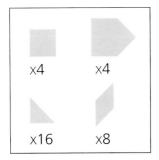

x4   x4

x16   x8

Before You Start

It's probably sensible to start with a small project, say a cushion or bag. Draw out your pattern full size on heavyweight paper and identify the shapes you're going to work with, for example hexagons or diamonds. Try using a traditional patchwork block – we've illustrated some suitable ones showing grid lines so that you can enlarge them to the size you want. Notice that templates for English Patchwork do not include a seam allowance, unlike those for American Patchwork which always include one. Make a master template for each shape by tracing it onto the cardboard or plastic, and cut it out accurately. Scissors are all right for cutting plastic, but cardboard is best cut with a sharp craft knife. Patchwork suppliers also sell a wide range of ready-to-use templates with which you can create your own patterns. Draw around your master templates on paper and cut out as many paper templates as you will need for each shape. The total number will depend on your particular project.

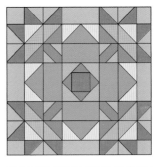

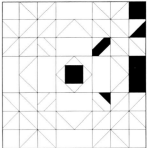

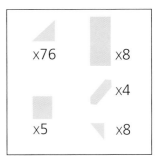

x76   x8

        x4

x5   x8

MAKING THE PATCHES AND BLOCKS

STEP 1 Lay a paper template on a piece of fabric and pin it in place. Cut out the fabric, leaving a good seam allowance all around the template.

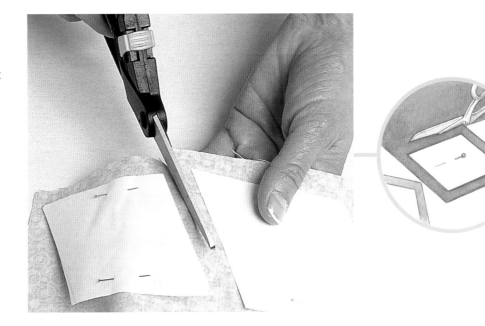

STEP 2
Fold the seam allowance over each edge of the paper and baste all round, turning in the fabric at the corners. Make sure you secure the corners by taking a small backstitch each time you come to one.

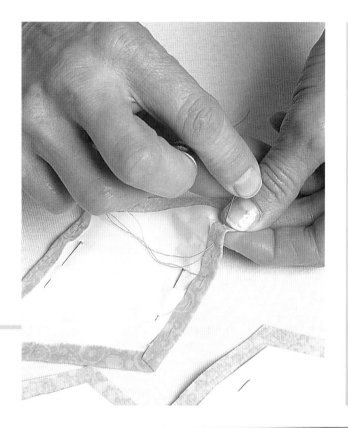

TIME-SAVER

If you need a lot of paper templates, you can cut out several at a time. Layer three or four papers together under the template, hold firmly in your left hand and run the scissors around the edge of the template.

STEP 3
Sew the patches together. Pass a knot in the thread, place two patches right sides together and bring the thread through from the back so that the knot is hidden in the turning. Whipstitch the edges with small, neat stitches. Finish each seam by making a few backstitches and then snipping off the thread.

TIME-SAVER

When working in blocks, it is easy to see how many papers you will need for each one. But when working on a larger project, such as a bedspread worked in only one shape, you may have to cut more paper templates as you proceed.

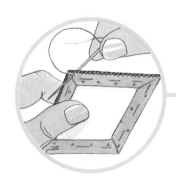

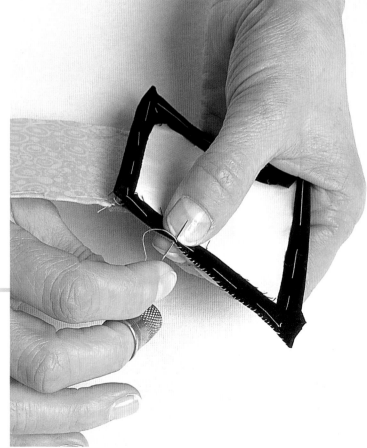

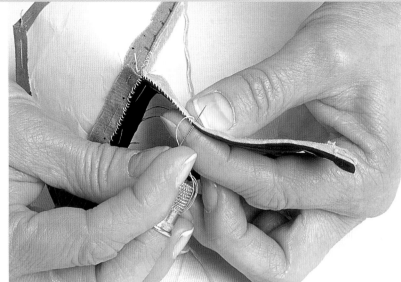

STEP 4
To fit a third patch into a tight angle, realign the patches but instead of continuing with the same thread, finish off the seam with a few backstitches, snip off the thread and start each seam again – you'll get a stronger seam that way.

STEP 5
When the patchwork is complete, take out the basting stitches, remove the paper patches and press gently. If you're careful in taking out the papers, you can reuse them.

TIP

You can have a lot of fun with strongly patterned fabric by using a window template. This is cut away in the middle so that you can place it on a specific part of the pattern and use just that section of the material for your patch. By choosing specific elements from the fabric and repeating them, new patterns can be created.

PROJECT 3:
TUMBLING BLOCKS CUSHION

Finished size: 53 x 58 cm (21 x 23 in)

master template

This striking three-dimensional design is pieced by hand over paper templates. It is made from a single template, a 60-degree diamond, joined in blocks to create a three-dimensional optical illusion. Notice that to achieve the full effect it is important to use three colours for each block: dark, medium and light. The cushion is easily made from cotton fabrics but can be transformed into a luxury item with a Victorian feel to it by including fabrics like silk and velvet.

WHAT YOU NEED

- Master template 60 degree diamond. The quantities of fabrics and measurements are based on a diamond with 7 cm (2¾ in) sides. Make one from cardboard as explained on page 17.
- Paper for templates.
- Small scraps of fabric in three colours: one dark, one light, one medium.
- Muslin backing fabric 56 x 61 cm (22 x 24 in)
- Cotton lining fabric for the back of

the cushion: 56 x 61 cm (22 x 24 in) – this can be plain or patterned.
- 57 g (2 oz) weight polyester batting 56 x 61 cm (22 x 24 in)
- Fabric for borders in a colour that tones or contrasts with the patchwork: four 7.5 x 61 cm (3 x 24 in) strips.
- Quilting thread in a neutral colour (it won't show, as it will be lost in the quilt 'sandwich').
- Pillow form.

INSTRUCTIONS

STEP 1 Make 16 patches
from each fabric. Follow the instructions for English piecing (pages 47–50) to make 16 blocks, each with a dark, a light and a medium fabric. To sew the blocks, use a neutral colour or one that will blend with the patches.

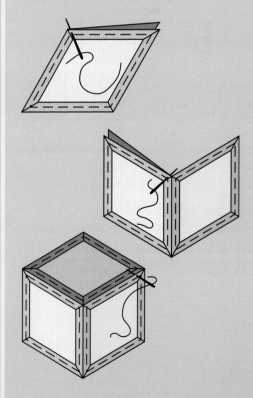

STEP 2 Join the blocks in rows.

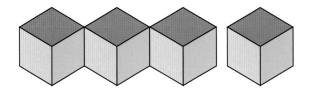

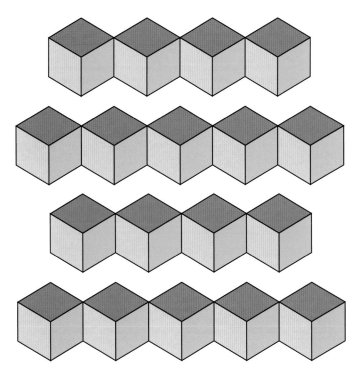

STEP 3 Join the rows together using the method described in English piecing. Remember to finish off the seam of each block before you 'pivot' the patches, then start the next seam.

STEP 4 Take out the basting stitches, remove the paper templates, and gently press the patchwork.

Measure the patchwork and add borders top and bottom. Measure again and add side borders. It's best to measure through the middle of the patchwork, not at the edges, which may stretch. If necessary, you can gently ease the edge to fit the border. Notice that sections of the side blocks will be cut off when the borders are attached.

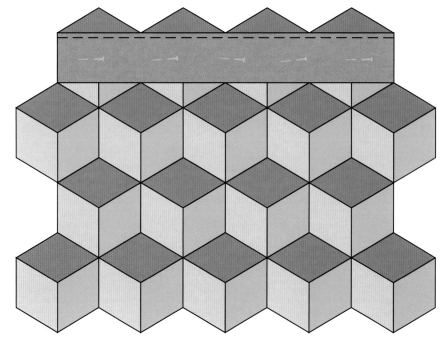

STEP 5
Lay out the backing fabric wrong side up and smooth it out well. Place the batting over it. Place the patchwork on the top, right side up. Make sure that there's plenty of overlap of batting and backing beyond the patchwork as it tends to shrink in the anchoring process. Pin the three layers together using long, glass-headed pins if you have them. Otherwise, you can anchor them with large basting stitches.

TIP

If you want to make your work more decorative, use embroidery floss in a complementary colour instead of quilting thread.

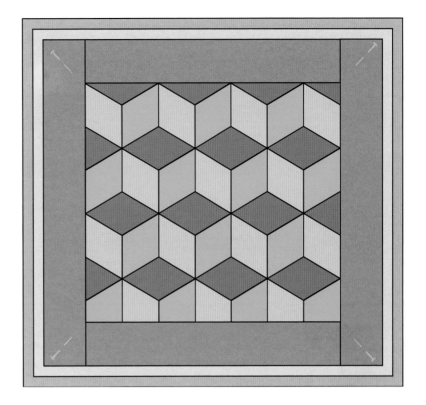

STEP 6
Using quilting thread, anchor the patchwork at the corners of the diamonds, passing the needle through all three layers and taking small backstitches. Cut off the thread at the back of the work.

Pull the needle through from the top of the cushion, leaving a 5 cm (2 in) 'tail.' Take two or three stitches in the same place, passing the needle right through all three layers. Finally, bring the needle to the surface and tie off, leaving the ends on show. Snip them off at about 2.5 cm (1 in) length.

STEP 7
To finish, lay the completed patchwork wrong side down on the lining. Trim all edges evenly. Stitch around all four sides, but leaving a large enough opening on the final side to insert the pillow form. Turn the work so that the patchwork is on the outside. Insert the pillow form and slipstitch the sides of the opening together.

USING A QUILTING HOOP

Instructions and tips for hand or machine quilting come with a health warning! It's all too easy, especially when starting out, to do too much quilting too quickly and end up with sore elbows, wrists and back. Repetitive strain injuries of this sort are very difficult to treat once the damage has been done. There are several measures you can take from the outset to avoid problems later on. Sit in a comfortable but firm chair that gives back support, both for hand and machine sewing. At regular intervals, pause and stretch your arms and back, and remember to flex your wrists and ankles.

Most important of all, limit the amount of time spent on one activity. Have several alternative tasks on hand, such as cutting out, quilting or pressing, so that you can move between them and not spend too long in one position.

The Quilting Stitch

The quilting stitch is a simple running stitch that passes through all three layers of the quilt 'sandwich'. Although it's possible to hand-quilt without using a frame or hoop, you'll get much better results if you learn how to use them. The basic idea is that the quilt 'sandwich' is held firmly and stretched out smoothly so that you can easily pass the needle through it.

If you're making a bed-sized quilt, a floor-standing frame is ideal and has the added advantage that the quilt 'sandwich' doesn't need to be basted. It also makes quilting easier on your back and joints as you can sit at a comfortable height without being tempted to slouch.

STEP 1 Follow the instructions in American Block Patchwork (page 34) to lay out the three layers of the quilt and pin together through all three layers. Baste the layers both up and down and then from side to side.

STEP 2 For small items, baste a border of spare fabric around all sides so that you can work easily on the pieced section.

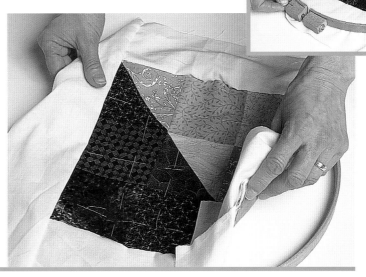

STEP 3 Working from the centre of the quilt, place the hoop's first ring under one section and press the hoop's second ring into position on top of the quilt. Check that the quilt is smooth on both sides. Set the tension so that it is firm but with enough give to allow the needle to pass easily through the layers.

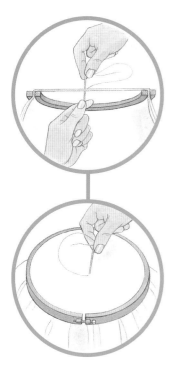

STEP 4
Make a knot in the end of the quilting thread and pull it up through the quilt from the back so that the knot pops through the backing and batting but not onto the surface. Take a small backstitch to anchor the thread, and begin making small running stitches, picking up two or three stitches at a time. The needle should go as straight down and up as possible. With the left hand under the quilt, press the fabric up and feel the tip of the needle as it comes through the sandwich. Try to make your stitches as even as possible, which is more important than how long they are.

TIME-SAVER

Try to develop a gentle rocking motion with the needle rather than pushing it hard. This will help you make stitches of an even length. A thimble with a ridge around the top will help, as you can lodge the end of the needle in it and just move it gently up and down.

STEP 5
When the section inside the hoop is completed, move the hoop to an adjacent section of the quilt.

The quickest and easiest method for quilting blocks is to quilt an 'outline' around each patch. Traditionally, the outline (or quilting line) is worked 0.5 cm (¼ in) away from the seam line (this is known as 'the quilter's quarter inch'). You don't need to mark the quilt, although to begin with you may like to use a pencil and ruler to mark in the line. You'll soon be able to 'eye-ball' the distance.

At the end of a line of quilting, take a small backstitch and run the thread between the layers, bring it to the back of the quilt, and snip off.

PROJECT 4:
RIBBON QUILT

Finished size: 198 x 137 cm (78 x 54 in)

This single size bed quilt of twenty-four blocks, hand quilted in a frame or hoop, would make an ideal quilt for a child or perhaps a gift for a young person going to university for the first time. The twenty-four blocks are set in six rows of four and produce an interesting 'lattice' effect when placed together. Don't be discouraged by the number of blocks to be pieced – they're really quick and easy. Practise your quilting skills on it to give the quilt the authentic homemade look that only hand quilting can produce. This is an ideal 'scrap' quilt, and you'll always get the lattice effect provided you place the dark and light fabrics as shown here.

Only two templates are needed for this quilt – a 11 cm (4½ in) square and a half square with sides a 11 cm (4½ in).

Note the placement of dark and light fabrics. If you are cutting the patches with scissors (rather than with a rotary cutter), make the templates first.

WHAT YOU NEED

- 1.25 m (1¼ yards) yellow fabric for stars
- 1 m (1 yard) dark fabric
- 1 m (1 yard) light fabric
- 1 m (1 yard) black fabric (for corner patches of each block)
- 1.5 m (1½ yards) border fabric
- 2 m (2 yards) backing fabric
- 2 m (2 yards) batting
- Hand-quilting thread
- Quilting needles ('betweens')
- Thimble
- Hoop or frame

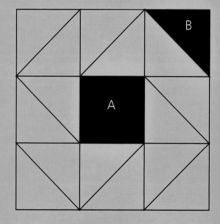

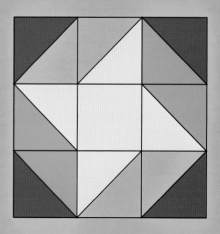

INSTRUCTIONS

STEP 1 Cut patches

as follows: 24 squares and 96 triangles of the yellow fabric, and 96 triangles of each of the dark, the light, and the black fabrics.

If you are using a rotary cutter, cut yellow squares from strips 11 cm (4½ in) wide. Cut triangles from strips 12 cm (4¾ in) wide.

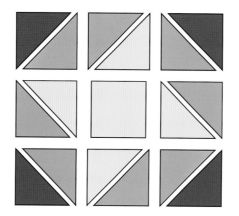

STEP 2 Piece the blocks as shown.

Check the measurements of the blocks, using a 32 cm (12½ in) square ruler if you have one.

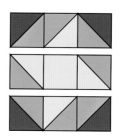
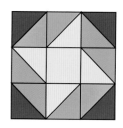

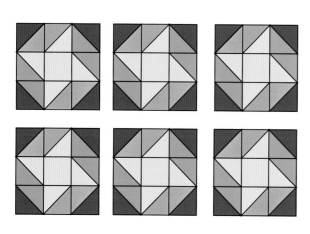

STEP 3 Join the blocks

in six rows of four, taking care to match the seams and to pin them before sewing.

TIME-SAVER

You can speed up the piecing progress by 'chain piecing' Line up the patches to be sewn together, then run them under the machine needle one after the other without snipping off the thread between the pairs of patches. Leave enough stitches between patches to allow you to snip them apart when you've finished.

STEP 4 Mitered borders

Measure the width of the quilt top and cut two 9 cm (3½ in) wide border strips of that length plus 18 cm (7 in). Pin one strip to the top of the quilt, placing the center of the border on the centre of the quilt, right sides together. Pin and stitch, but only up to the 0.5 cm. (¼ in) seam allowance at each end. Attach another strip to the bottom in the same way.

STEP 5 Open the

borders and measure the length of the quilt, including the newly added borders. Cut two 9 cm (3½ in) wide border strips of that length plus 18 cm (7 in). Attach to the sides, stitching only up to the 0.5 cm (¼ in) seam allowance as before.

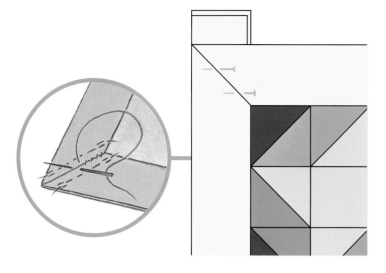

STEP 6

Lay the quilt top on a flat surface and allow the ends of the border strips to overlap. At each corner, turn the top strip under at an angle of 45 degrees, pin and baste (see page 32). Slipstitch the join, then turn to the back and cut off any excess fabric.

STEP 7

Quilting The style used in this quilt is 'outline' quilting (see page 56). Quilt around each patch 0.5 cm (¼ in) from the seam allowance. You may find it helpful to mark the quilting line with pencil when you start, but you'll soon be able to judge the distance by eye and won't need to mark it.

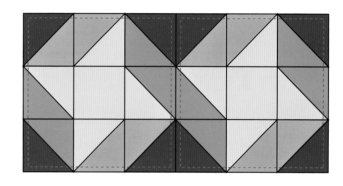

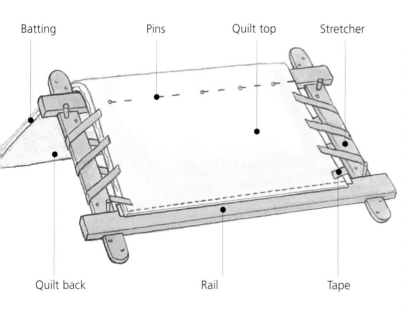

Batting   Pins   Quilt top   Stretcher

Quilt back   Rail   Tape

STEP 8

To quilt in a quilt frame The great advantage of this method is that you don't need to baste the quilt in advance. Place the edge of the backing on the front rail. Place the batting over the backing in the same way and pin to the burlap covering on the rail. Take the backing and batting over the back rail and let them hang over. Pin the edge of the quilt top over the backing and batting on the front rail and let that hang over the back also. Baste all three layers to the front rail. Pin the quilt to the back rail, making sure that all three layers are smooth and even. Adjust the tension by pinning tapes to the sides of the quilt and passing them around the side stretchers. Tension should be just firm enough to allow the needle to pass easily through the three layers using the correct rocking motion. As each section is completed, unpin the quilt from the back rail and roll it around the front rail so as to leave the next section ready for quilting.

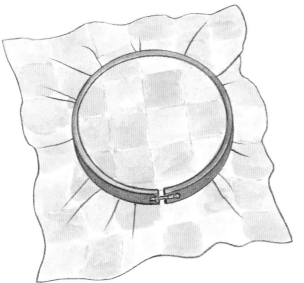

STEP 9

To quilt in a hoop Lay out the backing right side down on a flat surface and place the batting over it. Lay the quilt top right side up on top of the batting. Smooth out the layers and if possible anchor them by placing weights around the edges. Use long glass-headed pins to secure the three layers then baste, first horizontally and then vertically. When basting is complete, place a section of the quilt in a hoop, working from the centre out to the edges. When that section is completed, move to the next one.

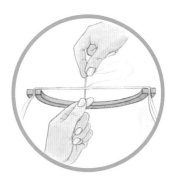

STEP 10

Finishing the quilt When quilting is complete, measure the width of the quilt through the centre and cut two 6 cm (2½ in) wide binding strips of this length. Fold in half with the wrong sides together. Then pin the binding strips to the top and bottom of the quilt on the right side, raw edges together. Stitch, using a walking (or even-feed) foot if you have one. Turn the binding to the back and slipstitch to the backing.

Measure the length of the quilt, again through the centre, and cut binding strips of this length plus 5 cm (2 in). Attach and sew as for the first two strips, neatening the ends by turning them in at the corners.

TIME-SAVER

Start basting from the centre of the quilt so as to minimize movement of the layers.

STEP 11

Last but not least, make a label and sew it to the back of your quilt.

Quilt As You Go

Sometimes, quilting a big quilt can seem a daunting prospect. It means having the time to spend on a concentrated period of quilting, which can be tiring and is hard on the wrists, elbows and back. It also means having the space to lay out, assemble and baste a quilt, which may not always be convenient. Here's a way to make quilts without any of those problems. Blocks are assembled with backing and batting as they are pieced, then quilted one at a time. When they're all completed they are joined to make the quilt. Another great advantage is that the work is portable – ideal to take on holiday or to pick up at odd moments. You make and quilt each block 'as you go', so at the end all you have to do is to join them and finish them and, hey presto – your quilt is done!

This technique is easy to work either by hand or machine. The important point to watch is that you don't quilt right up to the edge of the block. Leave a generous 0.5 cm (¼ in) seam allowance for joining the quilted blocks.

Quilt As You Go

What You Need
- Fabrics for whatever blocks you've chosen
- Backing fabric
- Batting
- Quilting thread (if you're sewing by hand)

Quilt As You Go

For each pieced quilt block, cut a piece of backing fabric and a piece of batting at least 2 cm (¾ in) larger all around than the block. Baste the block to the backing and batting as if it is a mini-quilt. Quilt by hand or machine, but remember not to quilt into the seam allowance around the edge of the block. Leave a generous 0.5 cm (¼ in) at all edges. When all your blocks are quilted, make them into a quilt like this:

STEP 1 Arrange the blocks in rows, with the backing facing up.

STEP 2 Pin the backing and batting back from the edges of the two blocks that are to be joined.

STEP 3 Pin the blocks right sides together, pinning and stitching through the quilt top only.

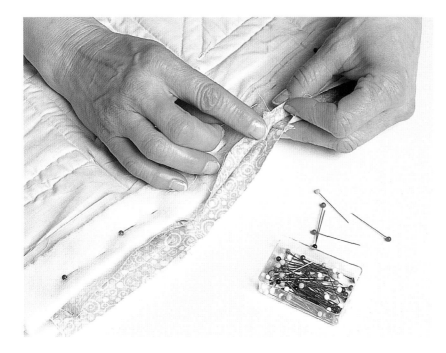

TIME-SAVER

Remember: if you are quilting by hand in a hoop, stitch a temporary border around the block so that the whole surface is available for quilting.

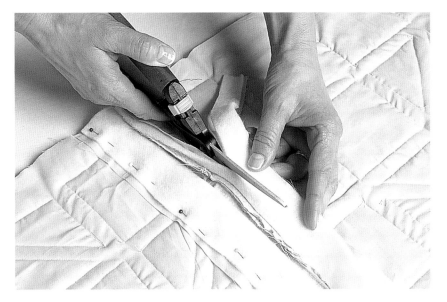

STEP 4 Unpin and trim back the batting on the first block.

STEP 5 Unpin and trim the batting on the other block so that the two edges meet. Slipstitch the edges of the batting together.

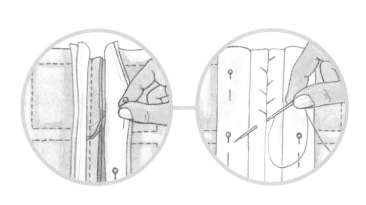

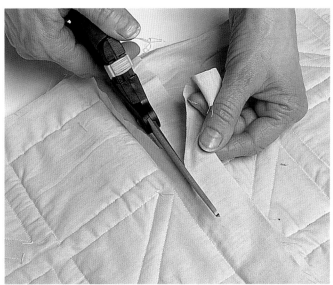

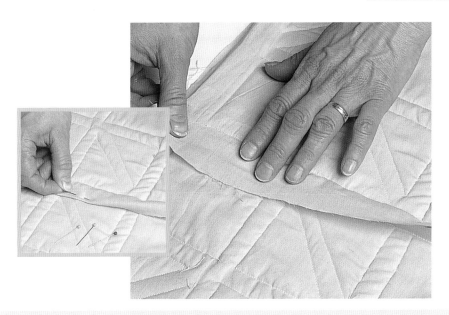

STEP 6 Carefully turn one side of the backing over the other, turn under and neatly slipstitch into position. To join the rows together, repeat this process until quilt is complete.

SEW AND FLIP

Sew and Flip is another popular technique and is the traditional way of making Log Cabin patchwork (see pages 72–74). It's also used for making Crazy patchwork, in which random scraps of fabric are stitched together, then embellished with fancy ribbons, embroidery and braid. Other patterns that work well with this method are Rail Fence, Roman Stripe and any 'string-pieced' blocks.

STEP 1
Cut background fabric from muslin or other thin fabric the same size as the finished block will be. Place a patch on the background fabric right side up, and pin into position.

STEP 2
Place another patch over the first patch, right sides together, and stitch with 0.5 cm (¼ in) seam allowance.

TIP

Instead of muslin background you can use paper, and tear it away when the stitching is finished. The paper should be firm but not too thick. When using a paper background it's best to use a slightly shorter stitch length than usual, to prevent the stitches from pulling away as you remove the paper.

STEP 3 Flip open
the second patch and press.
Continue in this way until the
block is complete.

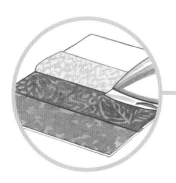

STEP 4 Turn to the back
of the block and trim the block
even with the foundation. Join
blocks with 0.5 cm (¼ in) seam
allowances.

SEW AND FLIP PLUS QUILT AS YOU GO

You can combine the Sew and
Flip technique with Quilt As You
Go to great effect.

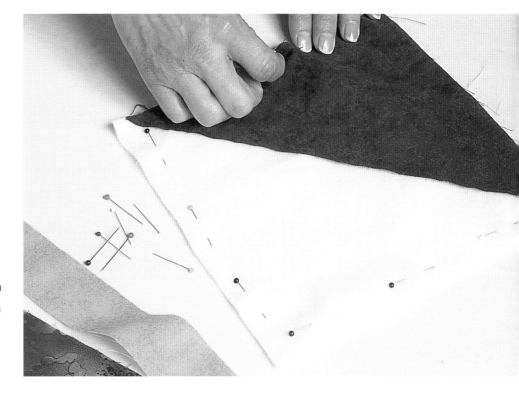

STEP 1 Cut a piece of backing
fabric and a piece of batting each 1.25 cm
(½ in) bigger all around than the block. Pin
them together around the edges. Place
the first patch on the batting and backing
and pin in position.

STEP 2
Place the second patch on the first one, right sides together, and pin and stitch through all the layers. Press the second patch open but take care to press lightly to avoid flattening the batting. Add the next patch in the same way.

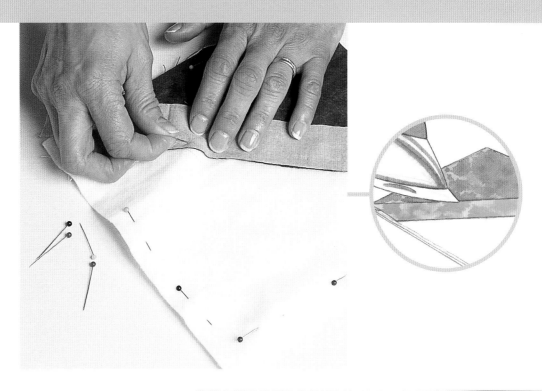

STEP 3
Proceed like this, stitching through all three layers each time, until the block is finished.

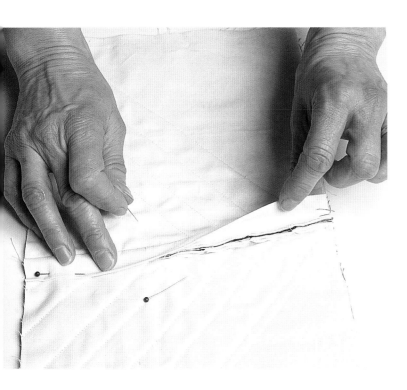

STEP 4
Trim the backing and batting even with the pieced top. Cut strips of backing fabric 6 cm (2½ in) wide. Fold the strips in half lengthwise. Place two blocks right sides together. Pin, then stitch the strip to the block edges, raw edges together, stitching through all the layers.

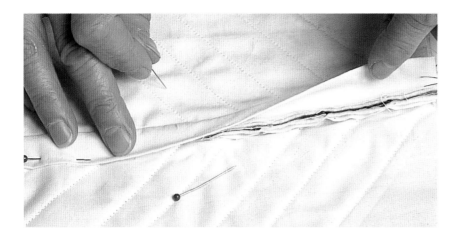

STEP 5
Fold the strip over the seam and neatly hem to the backing.

STEP 6
Join blocks in rows, then join the rows using the same method.

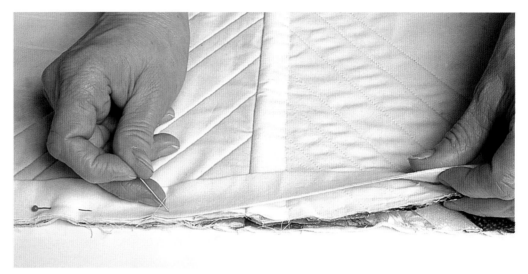

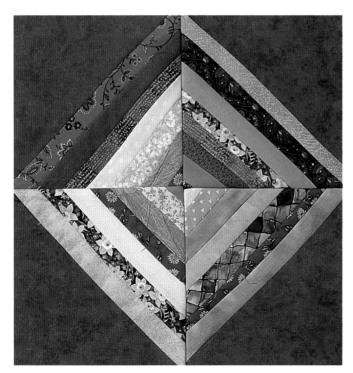

STEP 7
Press all seams on the back. Turn over and press the front of the block.

TIP

When combining Sew and Flip with Quilt As You Go, try to use the very thinnest batting available.

SCRAP-DASH STARS LAP QUILT

Finished size: (165 x 127 cm) 65 x 50 in

This lap quilt is made up from twelve 40 cm (16 in) blocks. Each block is pieced in four sections, making them very easy to handle and quick to piece. This design is a variation on the old-time 'string-piecing' technique, in which left-over scraps of fabric were cut into random strips, joined and used for piecing blocks. 'Scrap-dash Stars' is a creative way of using up fabrics left over from other projects. As well as being thrifty, you quilt each block as you make it, so all you need to do at the end is to join them – et voilà! – a completed quilt. Either choose fabrics and arrange them in colour groups, or make your blocks from completely random fabrics – either way will produce a pleasing effect. You can also arrange the blocks in different ways to make other patterns. Joining the blocks when they're finished is no problem using the method described in Quilt As You Go on page 61. If you piece these blocks on a foundation of paper or very thin fabric, this acts as a guide to the number of strips to use.

WHAT YOU NEED

- 1 m (1 yard) of fabric for the stars (choose either a very dark or a very bright fabric for this)
- Cotton scrap fabrics in a variety of colours – small and large scraps can be used
- 0.5 m (½ yard) fabric for binding
- Template for star rays
- Twelve 12 cm (8½ in) pieces of thin fabric or paper for foundation – use the foundation piecing 'stitch and tear' paper, tracing paper, or other thin paper. You can also use very fine fabric, such as fine muslin, which will be left in the blocks when finished
- 12 pieces of backing fabric each 43 x 43 cm (17 x 17 in)
- 12 pieces of batting each 43 x 43 cm (17 x 17 in)

INSTRUCTIONS

STEP 1 Cut up a quantity of scrap
fabrics in various colours in widths varying from 6 cm (2½ in) to 2.5 cm (1 in). Different lengths are fine.

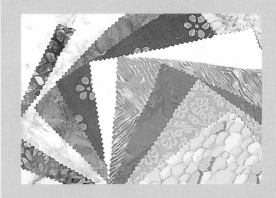

STEP 2
Make the template for the star rays by enlarging the shape shown right by 400 percent. Use the template to cut 48 patches from the star fabric.

Master template

STEP 3
Lay one star ray right side up diagonally across a foundation block, taking care to line up the corners at both ends as shown. Pin in position.

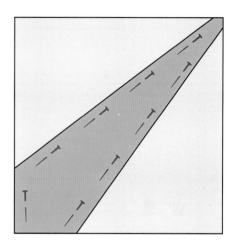

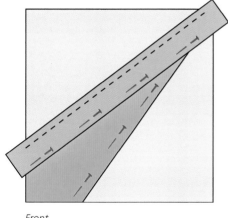

Front

STEP 4
Take a long rectangular strip and pin it right sides together on the star patch. Pin, then stitch, taking a 0.5 cm (¼ in) seam. Press the strip open. Repeat for the other side of the star patch.

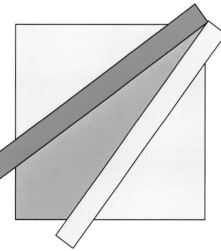

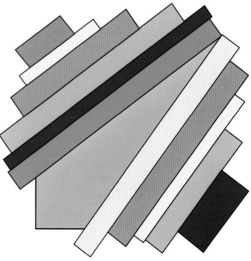

STEP 5
Take another strip and place it on the first one, right sides together, and stitch along the outer edge, again taking a 0.5 cm (¼ in) seam. Each strip must extend over the edge of the foundation. Repeat this, pressing each strip open as it's attached, until the foundation is completely covered. As you get towards the edge of the block you'll find you can use shorter strips. Repeat this process on the other side of the star ray.

STEP 6
Turn to the back of the block and with a ruler and rotary cutter, cut off the excess fabric, using the foundation paper or fabric as a guide. Make 48 blocks like this.

QUILT AS YOU GO

Now that you've made all the blocks, you can put them together with batting and backing.

STEP 1
Join four blocks so that they form a larger star block. Make 16 large blocks like this.

STEP 2
Lay out a piece of backing fabric right side down, then a piece of batting over it. Place the star block on top, right side up, and pin through all three layers.

TIP

If you draw this or any other patchwork pattern and photocopy it several times, you can use the grids to try out different colour schemes. Use coloured pencils or felt-tip pens depending on the intensity of colour that you want in the finished patchwork.

STEP 3
Stitch 'in the ditch' (page 43) through the centre of each block in both directions and around the stars, but stitch only to within 0.5 cm (¼ in) of the edge of the block. Quilt some of the other seams at regular intervals.

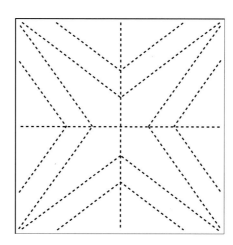

STEP 4
Quilt all of the star blocks like this.

ASSEMBLING THE BLOCKS

Look at the instructions for Quilt As You Go on pages 61–63.

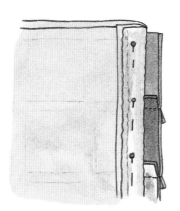

STEP 1
Trim the backing and batting so that the edges are even. Pin back both the backing and the batting, leaving the edges of the pieced top free.

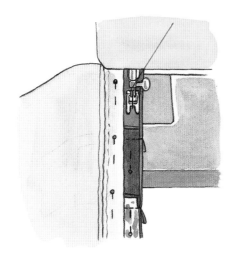

STEP 2
Place two blocks right sides together, pin, and then stitch with 0.5 cm (¼ in) seam. Turn to the back of the quilt and trim the batting so that the edges meet without overlapping.

STEP 3
Slipstitch the edges of the batting together. Smooth down the backing fabric of one block, leaving the edge rough. Fold the edge of the next block over it, and neatly slipstitch the fold over the rough edge.

STEP 4
Join blocks in rows like this, then repeat the process for joining the rows. Complete the quilt by binding the edges as explained on page 34.

LOG CABIN PATCHWORK

Log Cabin is one of the oldest and most popular of all traditional patchworking techniques. It combines the thrift of the scrap quilt with the potential to create striking graphic effects. Strips of fabric – the 'logs' – are stitched around a central square, that in folklore is said to represent the hearth in the log cabin, and which for this reason is usually bright red. The strips are dark on one side of the block, which is like the side of the room furthest away from the hearth, and light on the other side to reflect the firelight. This asymmetry means that the blocks can be arranged to produce a variety of patterns, each of which has a name. In Straight Furrow, for example, the quilt is striped horizontally or diagonally by dark and light stripes, while in Streak o' Lightning, the surface is covered by bold zigzags.

Choice of Foundation Materials

Log Cabin is a favorite block for scrap quilts because however many fabrics and colours are used, providing you keep the dark/light contrast on each side of every block, the patterns will still emerge when the blocks are set together. Traditionally, Log Cabin is worked over a foundation. The foundation provides stability and prevents the strips from moving and distorting in the sewing. Foundations can be either thin muslin, or any other fine fabric or paper. Fabric foundations are left in the block, but paper ones are torn away when stitching is finished.

If using paper foundations, the special quilting paper is best as it's easy to tear away without dragging on the stitches. In any case, remember to slightly reduce the length of stitches when stitching over paper.

To demonstrate this technique we've used a 30 cm (12 in) block but it can be adapted for any size you wish. Always draw the block out full size on squared paper to determine the size of the centre square and the width of strips needed.

LOG CABIN PATCHWORK USING BASIC FOUNDATION PIECING

WHAT YOU NEED

- Thin muslin or other fabric, or paper, for foundation
- 4 cm (1½ in) strips of dark and light fabrics
- Red (or other bright colour) for centre square

TIME-SAVER

For an easy way to make a light summer coverlet, use a thin muslin foundation and join the finished blocks in the usual way. Instead of quilting the top, simply line it and anchor the layers with ties. (See the project on page 38 for how to do this.) The foundation will give a little added solidity to the patchwork but the coverlet will be much lighter than a quilt.

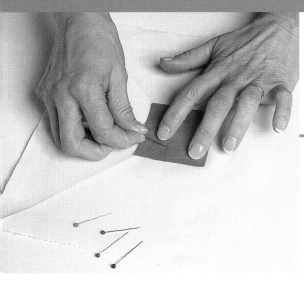

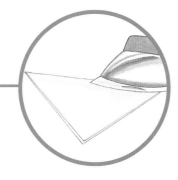

STEP 1
Cut a 30 cm (12 in) square of foundation. Iron the foundation to create the diagonal lines that will mark the centre of the block. Cut a 6 cm (2½ in) square of red fabric for the centre of the block. Place the red square, right side up, in the centre of the foundation piece, using the creases to line up the corners. Pin in position.

STEP 2
Cut a light strip 6 cm (2½ in) long and lay it on the square of red fabric, right sides together. Pin in position then stitch, taking a 0.5 cm (¼ in) seam allowance. Press the strip open.

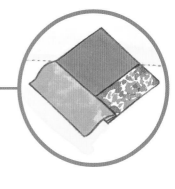

STEP 3
Cut another light strip 9 cm (3½ in) long and lay it across the first two patches, right sides together, pin and stitch. Continue like this, adding two light strips and two dark strips until there are four strips on each side of the block. Note that you must add 3.8 cm (1½ in) to the length of alternate strips as the block grows outward.

TIP

Instead of placing the light and dark strips on adjacent sides you can vary the block by placing them on opposite sides. This makes a block known as Courthouse Steps.

TIME-SAVER

An easy way to add the 'logs' without the trouble of measuring them is to cut each strip longer than needed, pin it to the block, and cut off the surplus. Then stitch in position.

STEP 4 To complete the block, press gently from the back and then the front. If necessary, trim the last round of strips even with the foundation fabric. If you're using paper as a foundation, remove it at this stage. When all the blocks are finished, lay them out and decide on the most pleasing arrangement.

LOG CABIN WITHOUT FOUNDATION

You can still work this sort of patchwork simply by adding the 'logs' around the centre square without using a foundation. The secret of success is to use really firm fabrics that won't distort at the edges, and to aim for complete accuracy with the seam allowances. Before starting, iron all the fabrics with starch to ensure crisp, even edges when you cut the strips. Press each strip as it's added, but take great care not to press too hard. As each round of 'logs' is completed, check the measurements and correct any inaccuracies at that stage.

PROJECT 6:
LOG CABIN QUILT

Finished size: 152 x 152 cm (60 x 60 in)

This striking bed-quilt or throw is made up from thirty-six 25 cm (10 in) machine-pieced blocks. The 'barn-raising' pattern is the ideal introduction to the ever-versatile Log Cabin style of quilt. It is made with only three light and three dark fabrics, plus some red for the centre squares and binding, but you can also make this pattern as a scrap quilt, using as many dark and light scraps as you like – so it's ideal for using up all those left-over fabrics from other projects! Look at the general instructions for the Log Cabin technique on pages 72–74 for more details about this. Of course, you can also vary the arrangement of the completed blocks, as described on page 74. The quilt is machine quilted in the seams between the blocks and with diagonal lines across the blocks, then finished with bound edges.

WHAT YOU NEED

- 27 cm (36 x 10½ in) foundation squares (thin interfacing or paper)
- 2 m (2 yards) of red fabric for the center squares and binding
- Light fabrics:
- Fabric 1: 0.4 m (⅜ yard)
- Fabric 2: 0.4 m (⅜ yard)
- Fabric 3: 1 m (1 yard)
- Fabric 4: 0.5 (½ yard)
- Fabric 5: 0.6m (⅝ yard)
- Fabric 6: 1 m (1 yard)
- Piece of batting 157 x 157 cm (62 x 62 in)
- Piece of backing fabric 157 x 157 cm (62 x 62 in)

INSTRUCTIONS

Note: all strips are cut 5 cm (2 in) wide.

STEP 1
Cut 36 foundation squares, each 27 x 27 cm (10½ x 10½ in) Press each square to make diagonal creases.

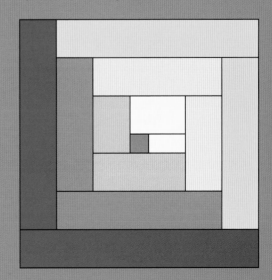

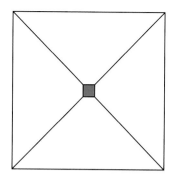 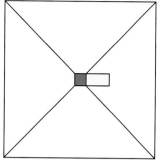

STEP 3 Cut a light strip 4 x 5 cm (1½ x 2 in) and place it right side down on the red square. Stitch, taking a 0.5 cm (¼ in) seam allowance. Open the strip out and press lightly. If you press too firmly the strips will tend to distort at the edges.

STEP 2 Cut 3.8 cm (1½ in) centre squares from the red fabric and place one exactly in the centre of the block, lining the corners up with the creases.

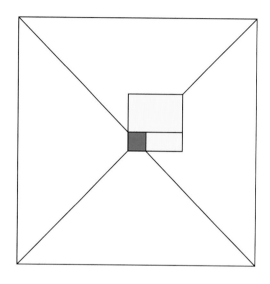

STEP 4 Cut a light strip 7.5 cm (3 in) long and place it right side down across the first two strips. Stitch in place, open, and press lightly as before.

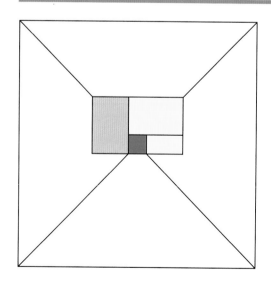 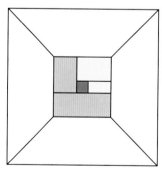 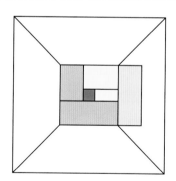

STEP 6 Cut a dark strip 11 cm (4½ in) long and add it to the block as before.

STEP 7 Cut and add a light strip 11 cm (4½ in) long.

STEP 5 Cut a dark strip 7.5 cm (3 in) long and stitch to the last two strips.

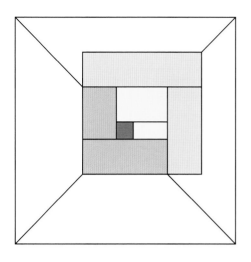

STEP 8

Cut and add a light strip 15 cm (6 in) long.

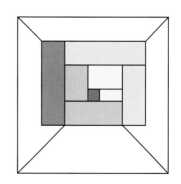

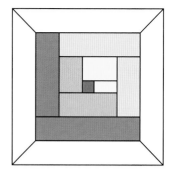

STEP 9 Cut and add a dark strip 15 cm (6 in) long; press.

STEP 10 Cut and add a dark strip 15 cm (6 in) long; press.

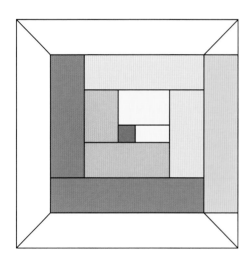

STEP 11 Cut and add a light strip 19 cm (7½ in) long.

TIP

Log Cabin quilts can be made in two or fifty colours; any fabric can be used; the strips may be any width you choose; and once several blocks are completed, they can be arranged in any number of different ways.

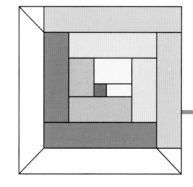

STEP 12 Cut and add a light strip 23 cm (9 in) long; press.

STEP 13 Cut and add a dark strip 23 cm (9 in) long; press.

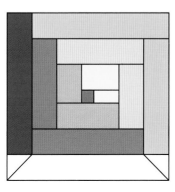

STEP 14 Cut and add a dark strip 27 cm (10½ in) long.

As each block is completed, check that it measures 27 cm (10½ in). Trim if necessary. If you have used paper foundations, remove them now.

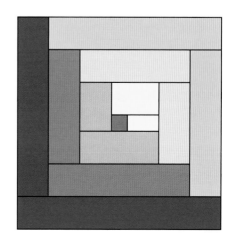

MAKING UP THE QUILT

STEP 1 Lay out all the blocks on a flat surface in rows of six, rotating them in order to create the barn-rasing pattern as shown below. Look at the diagram for the exact arrangement.

STEP 2 Pin and join the blocks in six rows of six blocks. Pin and join the rows.

STEP 3 Lay out the backing and batting, and assemble the quilt for basting and quilting, following the instructions on page 31.

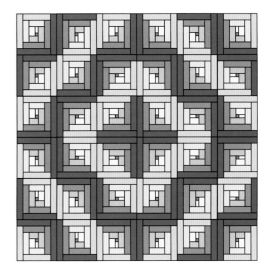

STEP 4 Pass the quilt under the machine needle, roll the right-hand side of it, and secure it with clips. Use a walking foot if possible. Stitch 'in the ditch' (page 43) along all the seams between the blocks.

STEP 5 Remove the quilt from the machine and mark diagonal lines on each block using a 2B pencil or chalk marker. Follow the marked lines to quilt all the blocks.

STEP 6 To finish the quilt, measure it through the centre – it should measure 154 cm (60½ in) in both directions. If there are any errors, simply ease the edges to fit the binding, which will ensure that your quilt lies flat. Cut two 6 cm (2½ in) strips of binding fabric 154 cm (60½ in) long. Fold in half, wrong sides together, then pin and stitch to the opposite sides of the quilt. Fold to the back and slipstitch to the backing. Cut two 6 cm (2½ in) strips 159 cm (62½ in) long and attach to the other two sides, turning in the excess at each end to neaten the corners.

HAND QUILTING

HAND QUILTING

WHAT YOU NEED

- Quilting needles – 'betweens'
- Quilting thread
- Hoop or frame (see page 54)
- Templates or stencils
- 2B pencil or other marker
- Fabric eraser

Nothing can compare with hand quilting to give a quilt that authentic look that we all associate with the traditional patchwork quilt. Of course, not all old quilts were quilted with small, beautifully neat, even stitches. Many of them were quilted in a purely functional way, no doubt with the idea of getting a much-needed bed covering into use as quickly as possible. Many tales are told of the old-times when groups of women got together to quilt the pieced tops that they'd accumulated. It wasn't just a business meeting either – it was an important social event, an excuse for fun and socializing in hard-working rural communities.

Traditions of Hand Quilting

The art of hand quilting combines the functional purpose of anchoring the layers of a quilt together, and decorating the surface. It's one of the oldest textile traditions in the world. Some of the finest examples of hand quilting are seen on the wholecloth quilts that are the traditional style of the quilts made in the North of England. They are called North Country quilts, or sometimes Durham quilts. Wholecloth quilts are not pieced, like patchwork quilts, but made of a single piece of fabric, which may be plain or patterned, that is quilted with a variety of quilting patterns, many of them passed down through the generations.

In America, also, certain regions have developed characteristic styles of hand quilting. Most notably, the Amish people of Pennsylvania produce quilts that combine striking graphic effects created by the use of bold, simple geometric shapes pieced in strong colours, with superb hand quilting. Today, American quilters bring their own standards of excellence and beauty to the art of hand quilting.

To become a really expert quilter takes time and practice, but everyone has to start somewhere and the best way is to get a grasp of the basics and then develop your skills from there.

In Using a Quilting Hoop (page 54) we covered very simple hand quilting in which patchwork is outlined with quilting. Let's look at some more sophisticated methods that will enable you to enhance any quilted item with patterns that you can copy or design yourself.

MARKING THE QUILT TOP

You must mark the chosen pattern on the quilt top before it is assembled for quilting. If you are working on a fairly light-coloured quilt top, it's possible to place patterns under the top and trace over them.

STEP 1
Lay the top out on a table or other flat surface with the quilting pattern under it. Small items can be pinned over the pattern. For larger quilts, first anchor the pattern to the table using masking tape. Place the quilt top over it and anchor that down as well. Alternatively, weigh it down around the edges with books or other heavy items. If the quilt top stretches to the edges of the table, you can use bulldog clips to secure it to the edges. The idea is to keep the quilt top as smooth and taut as possible. Make sure your patterns are well outlined in dark pen or marker so that they show up through the top.

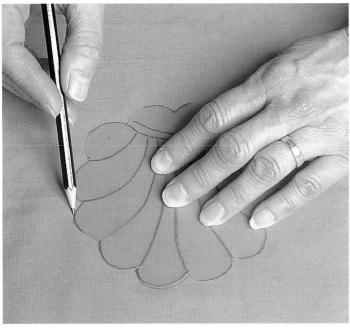

STEP 2
Using stencils is an alternative way of marking on fabric. Use a 2B pencil, a quilter's silver pencil, or any washable quilter's marker that can easily be removed after quilting.

TIME-SAVER
If you have trouble seeing the pattern lines through dark fabrics, you can use a glass surface (for example a glass-topped table) with a lamp underneath it, or a lightbox if you have one. Another alternative is to fix the pattern and the quilt top to a window, using adhesive tape, so that the lines show through.

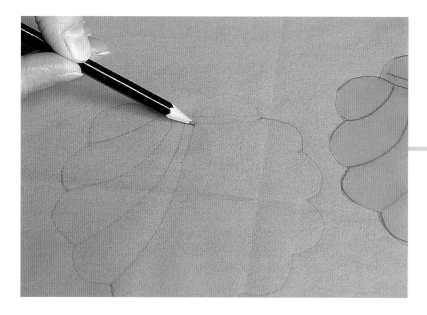

STEP 3
Once you've drawn around the outline of the stencil, you can draw in some of the lines freehand. When marking is complete, assemble the quilt with backing and batting and baste it, as described on page 34.

STEP 4
Place the quilt sandwich (the three layers of the quilt) in a hoop or frame. Use the side screw to adjust the tension so that the needle can be moved up and down easily through the layers.

TIP
Long periods of quilting may cause the finger underneath the quilt to become sore. Special finger-guards can be purchased, or you can use plasters as long as they're thin enough for you to still feel the point of the needle as it comes through.

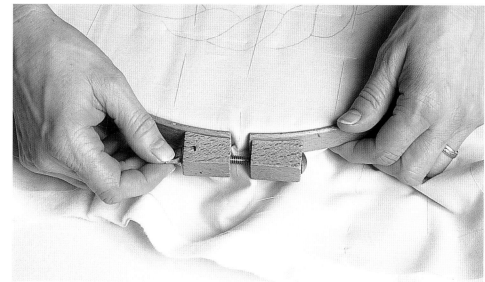

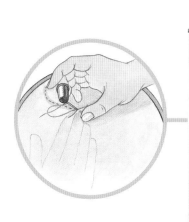

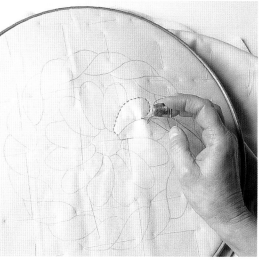

STEP 5
Using the quilting stitch described on page 54, quilt over the marked lines. The needle should pass through the layers at as straight an angle as possible. Using the middle finger to push up from underneath, gather three or four stitches on the needle before pulling it through. You should just be able to feel the point of the needle underneath as it comes through.

AMISH-STYLE WALL QUILT

Finished size: 96 x 96 cm (38 x 38 in)

This handsome Amish-style wall-quilt is designed to showcase your hand-quilting skills. It is a scaled-down version of an authentic Lancaster County quilt, accurately reflecting the colours, style and quilting patterns traditionally used in such quilts. Even to this day, the Amish, or Plain People as they call themselves, maintain their austere lifestyle, rooted in their religious beliefs and rural traditions. Their quilts are generally pieced from large patches in strong, saturated colours, the striking effect of the piecing being enhanced by the beautifully worked hand-quilting designs with which they are decorated. The quick and easy piecing means that you can relax and take your time over the quilting. Choose cotton fabrics in solid, strong colours and contrasting quilting threads if you want to highlight the quilting patterns.

WHAT YOU NEED

Note: 'fat quarters' are pieces measuring approximately 48 x 48 cm (19 x 19 in)

- 1 fat quarter of red fabric
- 2 fat quarters of purple fabric
- 0.5 m (½ yard) green fabric
- 1.5 m (1½ yards) black fabric for the backing and binding
- Batting 100 x 100 cm (39 x 39 in)
- Quilting 'betweens' needles
- Quilting thread

INSTRUCTIONS

STEP 1 Cut the
following patches: From the red fabric – one 27 cm (10½ in) square and four 6 cm (2½ in) squares. From the purple fabric – four strips, each 6 x 26 cm (2½ x 10½ in) and four 27 cm (10½ in) squares. From the green fabric – four 37 x 27 cm (14½ x 10½ in) pieces.

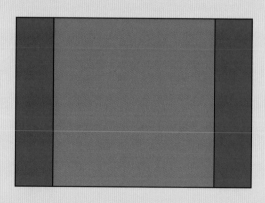

STEP 2 Pin, then stitch a purple strip to opposite sides of the red square.

STEP 3
Pin a red square to each end of the other two purple strips. Then attach these strips to each of the other sides of the red square, carefully matching and pinning the seams before you stitch.

STEP 4
Pin and stitch a green patch to the top and bottom of the centre square. Join a purple square to each end of the two remaining green patches.

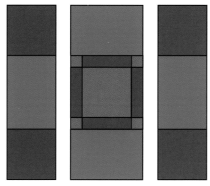

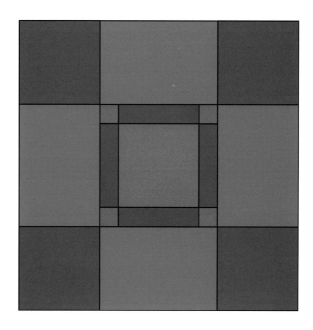

STEP 5
Pin and join the green and purple strips to the centre square, one on each side.

QUILTING

The full pattern is given for the centre square. The corner pattern is repeated four times. The centre square pattern should measure 35 x 35 cm (13¾ x 13¾ in).

Corner pattern template (left) and centre square pattern template (above).

STEP 1
Enlarge the corner pattern shown left by 600 percent. Trace out both patterns full size on heavyweight paper. Go over the lines with a marking pen. Then anchor the design on a flat surface with masking tape.

STEP 2
Place the quilt top over the design and anchor as before. Carefully trace the design on to the quilt top, using either a soft 2B pencil, chalk marker or quilter's silver pencil. If the design doesn't show through strongly enough, try one of these methods:

- Fix the design to a window with Scotch tape and place the quilt top over it, anchoring it with masking tape. Now the design will show through clearly and be easy to trace.
- Make your own light box (if you don't already have one) by placing a lamp under a glass-topped table. Alternatively, you could buy a sheet of glass from a DIY shop and support it on books.

STEP 3
From black fabric, cut backing 100 x 100 cm (39 x 39 in). The extra fabric allows for shrinkage caused by the quilting. Lay out the backing, then the batting, and finally the quilt top, pinning and basting as described on page 34.

STEP 4
Baste a temporary muslin border around the entire quilt; this will enable you to quilt the edges.

STEP 5
Place the quilt in a hoop (see page 54) and begin quilting from the centre. Remember: the best way to achieve even quilting stitches is to use a rocking movement as you gather up the stitches on the quilting needle.

STEP 6
When all the quilting is complete, remove the muslin border and neaten the edges by trimming back the backing and batting to the edge of the quilt top.

BINDING

The Amish style of binding is slightly different from the method demonstrated on page 34.

STEP 1

Cut two 11 x 94 cm (4½ x 37 in) wide strips of binding fabric. Fold each strip in half lengthwise, wrong sides together, and pin strips to the top and bottom of the quilt. Fold the binding double again, and take the folded edge over to the back of the quilt. Hemstitch to the backing.

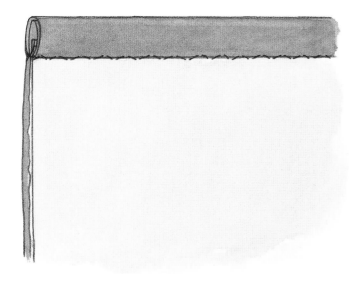

STEP 2

Cut two 11 x 97 cm (4½ x 38 in) strips of binding fabric. Attach evenly to the other two sides of the quilt as shown in Step 1, leaving enough at each end to turn under and neaten the corners.

STEP 3

Finally, attach a hanging sleeve. From the backing fabric, cut a strip 20 x 86 cm (8 x 34 in). Fold it in half lengthwise, wrong sides together and stitch the raw edges together, leaving a 0.5 cm (¼ in) seam allowance. Press the seam open so that it is in the middle of the strip. Turn in at each end and stitch. Pin the sleeve to the back of the quilt below the binding, and then slipstitch to the backing.

TIP

Be careful about using too much black in your quilt as black absorbs light, giving patterns a more intense but somber feel.

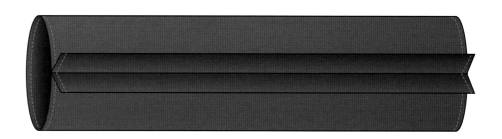

SEMINOLE PATCHWORK

Chevrons

Chequerboard

Squares on point

Strip piecing is a quick and easy way to make lots of patchwork patterns, from simple chequerboards to 'on point' diamonds and chevrons. The basic technique involves nothing more difficult than stitching strips of fabric together, cutting them into segments, and rejoining them. It's often referred to as Seminole patchwork because it was developed by the Seminole Indians of the Florida Everglades, who used it to decorate their clothes.

Traditional Seminole patchwork is usually worked on a very small scale but the basic technique can be worked at any scale you choose. You can produce a variety of patterns depending on how many strips and colours you use, and it's one of the most popular and useful methods of making interesting quilt borders. This is essentially a machine-sewn method although it can be worked by hand if you're careful. Using a rotary cutter and mat will certainly make it easier to achieve neat and accurate patchwork.

Success with strip piecing begins with really accurately cut and joined strips, so check the 0.5 cm (¼ in) seam allowance on your machine. To get the most striking effects from the patterns, choose fabrics in colours that contrast well. Cut all strips on the straight grain of the fabric.

SEMINOLE PATCHWORK

WHAT YOU NEED
- Fabrics of contrasting colours
- Fabric scissors
- Sewing machine
- Rotary cutter and ruler
- Pins
- Cutting mat

TIME-SAVER

For this patchwork use the very thin, flower-headed pins that you can leave in place as you sew. The needle will run over them without breaking.

CHEQUERBOARD

To make a simple chequerboard by this method use two fabrics of contrasting colours.

STEP 1 Cut two strips from each fabric. The strips should be the same width as your finished squares will be, plus 1.25 cm (½ in) for the seam allowances – for example, for 7.5 cm (3 in) finished squares, cut 9 cm (3½ in). strips. Join the strips by placing right sides together and sewing with a 0.5 cm (¼ in) seam allowance to make a band of alternating colours.

STEP 2 Press the patchwork from the back. Press seams to one side. Press towards darker fabric to avoid it showing through the lighter one. Using a rotary cutter and ruler, neaten one end of the band and cut even segments each 9 cm (3½ in) wide.

STEP 3 Arrange the segments to create the chequerboard effect. Pin and stitch them together in rows. The pinning must be done carefully to ensure that the seams fit neatly. Finger-press and then pin the seams so that they lie in opposite directions at the joins.

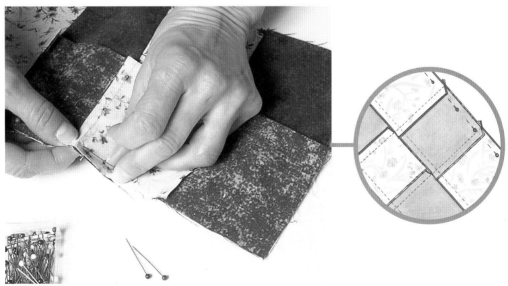

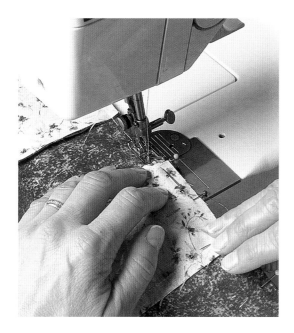

STEP 4 Machine stitch the rows together.

STEP 5 Press the patchwork from the back, pressing the seams to one side. Turn to the front and press again.

SQUARES ON POINT

Strips of diamonds, or 'on point' squares, are useful for quilt borders, decorating garments, and many other purposes. To make them, use one dark and one light fabric. The dark fabric will be the diamond.

STEP 1 Cut dark fabric strips according to the size you want your diamonds to be, for example 9 x 9 cm (3½ x 3½ in) strips for a 7.5 cm (3 in) finished diamond. Cut two strips from light fabric exactly 1.25 cm (½ in) wider than the dark fabric. Join the three strips with the dark fabric in the centre. Cut segments the same width as the dark fabric.

STEP 2
Lay out the segments, dropping one square down each time. Carefully match and pin the seams, and then join the segments by placing the right sides together and stitching with a 0.5 cm (¼ in) seam allowance.

STEP 3
Trim off the excess fabric at the top and bottom of the band to give a straight line, being sure to leave a 0.5 cm (¼ in) seam allowance on each side.

TIP

When pressing patchwork at the back of a piece of work, always press the seams towards darker fabric to avoid it showing through the lighter one.

CHEVRONS

Chevrons make another interesting effect. To make a chevron pattern by the same method, two contrasting fabrics are needed: fabric A and fabric B.

STEP 1 Cut one strip of fabric A wide. Cut two strips of fabric B 6 cm (2½ in) wide. Join the strips with fabric A in the middle to make a band as shown. Make two bands like this, then lay one on top of the other, wrong sides together. Pin carefully to make sure the centre seams meet. Use the 60 degree guide on your cutting mat, to cut 6 cm (2½ in) wide segments at that angle.

STEP 2 Lay out segments, alternating them to create the chevrons, then stitch them together.

STEP 3 Finally, trim the top and bottom of the pieced band, leaving 0.5 cm (¼ in) seam allowance on both sides.

QUILTER'S BAG

Finished size: 64 x 50 cm (25 x 20 in)

Every quilter needs bags for carrying tools, equipment and fabrics. This strip-pieced tote bag is specially designed with pockets to hold scissors, rulers, cutter and mat, with plenty of room left for fabrics. Your bag will soon become an indispensable accessory, and its striking patterns, with squares-on-point on one side and chevrons on the other, will catch everyone's eye. It is designed to take a standard 43 x 58 cm (17 x 23 in) cutting mat, which is a practical size both for carrying around and for home use. Follow the instructions for making up patchwork for both sides as if they were separate 'mini-quilts', then assemble and make the bag as described. Look back at Seminole Patchwork (pages 86–90) for instructions on the strip-piecing technique.

WHAT YOU NEED

Note: 'fat quarters' are pieces measuring approximately 46 x 46 cm (18 x 18 in).

- For the front: one fat quarter each of three different fabrics A, B and C
- For the back: one fat quarter each of two different fabrics D and E
- 0.5 m (½ yard) of fabric for borders, handles, and binding
- Two pieces of strong calico, each measuring 53 x 68 cm (21 x 27 in), for the lining of the bag
- 0.5 m (½ yard) of strong calico for the pockets
- Two pieces of thin batting, each measuring 53 x 68 cm (21 x 27 in)
- 15 cm (6 in) strip of stick-on Velcro
- 7.5 x 48 cm (3 x 19 in) stiff interfacing for handles

INSTRUCTIONS

FRONT OF BAG – SQUARES ON POINT

STEP 1 Cut six 6 cm (2½ in) wide strips of fabric A. Cut three 6 cm (2½ in) wide strips of fabric B. Join the strips in bands of three, with fabric B in the middle. Trim off the end from each strip, and cut them into 6 cm (2½ in) wide segments.

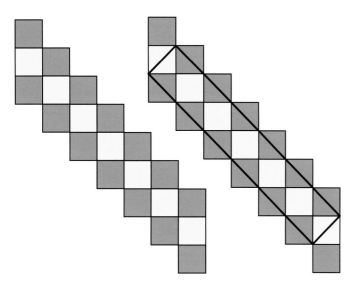

STEP 2
Join the segments in rows of seven, dropping down one strip at a time, to form a band (see page 89). Make three bands like this. Trim the bands top and bottom, leaving 0.5 cm (¼ in) seam allowances. Trim each each band evenly at both ends so that they measure exactly 39 cm (15½ in).

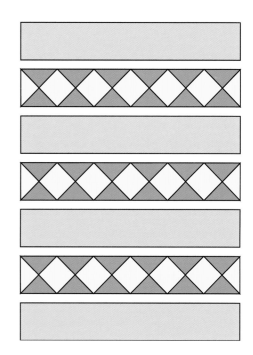

STEP 3
Cut four 6 x 39 cm (2½ x 15½ in) strips from fabric C. Join alternate pieced strips and fabric C strips.

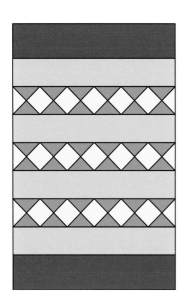

STEP 4
Cut two 7.5 x 39 cm (3 x 15½ in) strips from the border fabric. Pin right sides together to the top and bottom of the patchwork, and stitch in place. Press the borders open.

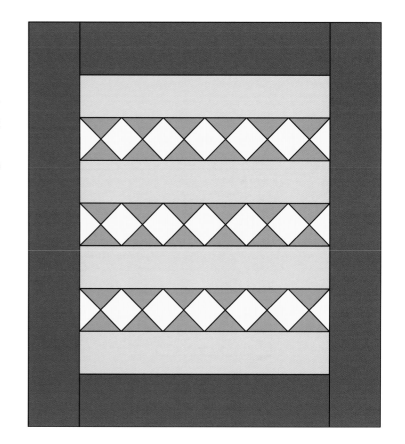

STEP 5
Cut two 7.5 x 65 cm (3 x 25½ in) strips from border fabric. Pin and stitch to the sides of the patchwork. Press these open.

BACK OF BAG – CHEVRONS

STEP 1
Cut one 6 x 47 cm (2½ x 18½ in) strip of fabric D. Cut two 6 x 47 cm (2½ x 18½ in) strips of fabric E. Join the three strips to make a band, with fabric D in the middle. Press seams towards the darker-coloured fabric. Fold the band in half, with the short edges together, carefully matching the seams. Pin at top and bottom of the band. Use a quilter's ruler or a cutting mat, to cut four 6 cm (2½ in) segments at an angle of 45 degrees to the horizontal.

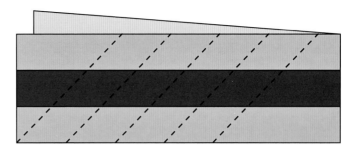

STEP 2
When you separate the two layers, you'll have segments at two angles which, when joined, make the chevron pattern. Join the segments in a row.

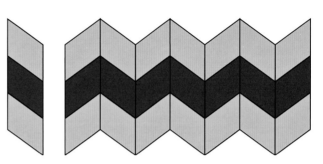

STEP 3
Trim the band evenly at top and bottom of the chevrons. Check that the band measures 11 cm (4½ in) wide. Trim it to 39 cm (15½ in) long.

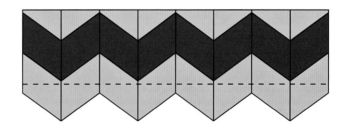

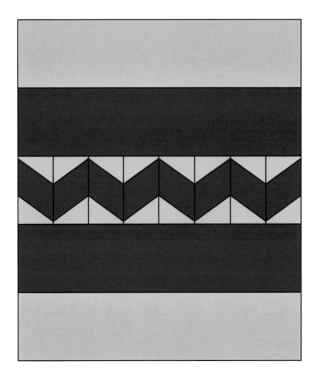

STEP 4
Cut two 11 x 39 cm (4½ x 15½ in) bands from each of fabric D and fabric E. Join the strips in this order: fabric D, fabric E, pieced chevrons band, fabric D, fabric E.

STEP 5
Make borders around the patchwork as described above for the front of the bag.

TIME-SAVER
Accuracy is of vital importance in Seminole Patchwork. Time spent measuring and cutting accurately will reap rewards later. The original strips must be cut and joined accurately and angled strips cut very carefully so that they are all at exactly the same angle.

ASSEMBLING THE BAG

STEP 1
For each patchwork panel, lay out the calico lining fabric. Place the batting on it and the patchwork on top, right side up. Pin, then baste all over.

STEP 2
Stitch each panel 'in the ditch' (see page 43). Trim off the edges of the batting and backing.

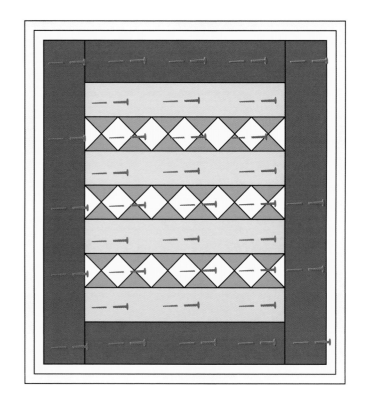

STEP 3
Make the four pockets. Enlarge the template for the scissors pocket (see below) by 150 percent. Cut two layers of fabric and stitch all around, leaving the bottom open. Turn the pocket inside out through the bottom opening, and close the opening with slipstitches.

STEP 4
For the second pocket, cut a piece of calico 21 x 21 cm (8½ x 8½ in). Fold in half and complete as for the first pocket. (This is the pocket for the rotary cutter.)

Scissor-pocket template

TIME-SAVER

Monofilament thread, also known as 'invisible thread', is ideal for quilting along the seams.

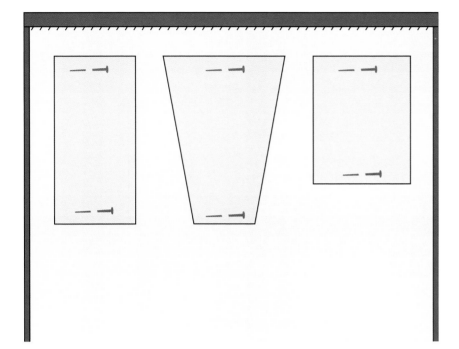

STEP 5
For the third pocket, cut a piece of calico 25 x 16 cm (10 x 6½ in). Fold in half lengthwise and complete as for the first pocket. (This is the pocket for notions – threads, needles and pins).

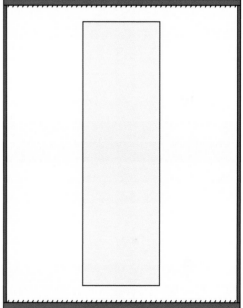

STEP 6
On the inside of the bag's front panel, position these three pockets 3 cm (1¼ in) below the top and spaced evenly. Pin into position, then hand stitch them to the lining with small, secure hemming stitches. Fix the strip of stick-on Velcro to the inside of the bag and to the top of the notions pocket to seal it.

STEP 7
Make the fourth pocket for the ruler. Cut calico 58 x 35 cm (23 x 14 in) and complete as above. Stitch the pocket to the inside lining of the bag's back panel.

HANDLES

STEP 1
Cut two strips of border fabric measuring 11 x 89 cm (4½ x 35 in). Cut two strips of interfacing 5 x 89 cm (2 x 35 in). Lay one strip of interfacing on one side of a handle strip 0.5 cm (¼ in) from the edge and baste.

STEP 2
Fold the handle strip in half with right sides together. Turn up the bottom edge over the interfacing, turn the top edge over it and stitch. Leave the ends open. Sew parallel lines along the handle to strengthen it.

STEP 3
Pin the handles to the outside of each panel with raw edges together. Cut two 7.5 x 51 cm (3 x 20 in) strips of binding fabric and fold in half lengthwise with wrong sides together. Pin one each to the top of the front and back panels of the bag and stitch. Taking a 1.25 cm (½ in) seam, stitch across the top of the bag and the handles.

STEP 4
Turn binding strips to the inside, and stitch to the lining.

FINISHING

STEP 1
Pin the back and the front of the bag together and baste all round. Cut 9 cm (3½ in) strips of binding fabric and join them to make one long strip 190 cm (75 in) long. Fold in half and then attach to the sides and bottom of the bag, starting at the top, leaving enough extra at each end to turn under neatly. Make a tuck as you turn each of the bottom corners (see right, below).

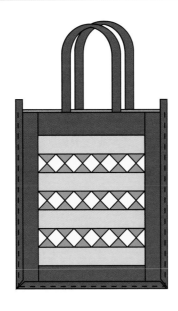

STEP 2
Fold the binding over the seam, and hem down to the other side. Fold the corners to make a mitre, and turn under the ends of the binding neatly at the top of the bag.

And that's it – a strong, practical bag that will give years of service.

MACHINE QUILTING

Machine quilting has become more and more popular as sewing machines have become more sophisticated – and as quiltmakers leading busier and busier lives want to speed up the quilting process. As a result machine quilting has developed as an art in its own right and many examples of the beautiful effects it can achieve are now seen at quilt shows and exhibitions.

Keys to Success

Many people find the idea of machine quilting rather challenging at first, but it really is just a case of learning some basic skills and then practicing them. Perhaps the most important thing is to really get to know your sewing machine and learn how to get the best out of it for quilting. Check that your machine is in good condition and properly oiled and maintained. In particular, make sure there is no fluff or lint in and around the bobbin case.

Make life as easy as possible by using the correct materials. To begin with, concentrate on cotton fabrics for top and backing. Use good-quality batting – cotton or a polycotton mix are suitable. Needle-punched or other flat, thin battings are easiest to work with.

The two basic types of machine quilting are straight machine quilting, for any patterns that can be stitched in straight lines or gentle curves, and free machine quilting for patterns with more exaggerated curves.

Before You Start

Before starting on your quilt, make some samples. This is important, as the last thing you want is to start quilting a sizeable item and run into problems with tension or stitch size. Time spent making some quick and easy samples is never wasted. Make two or three quilt sandwiches (top, batting, backing) of, say, 25 cm (10 in) square, and baste them well. If possible, use the same fabric, backing and batting as you have used in your quilt top.

Prepare your machine by attaching a walking foot, if using one, and set the needle tension slightly looser than usual. Set the stitch length at about 10 stitches per inch (2.5 cm).

STEP 1 Place a hand on either side of the portion to be quilted and press down gently but firmly. Quilt straight lines and check that the tension is correct (check back and front) and that the fabric isn't puckering up. Quilt across the first lines to make squares and again check for puckering and dragging. Adjust tension and stitch length until you're happy with the result.

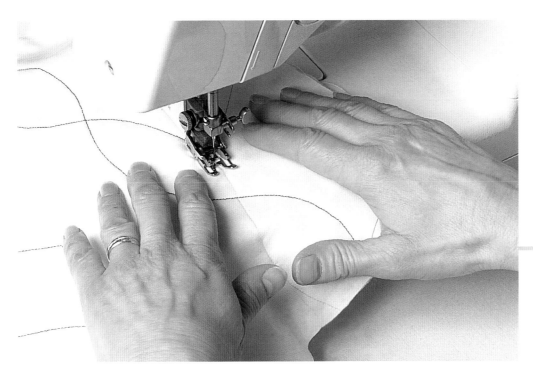

STEP 2 Practise quilting some gentle curves.

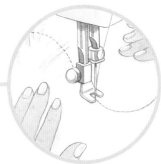

STEP3
Start and end each row with a couple of backstitches. When stitching is complete, thread the ends through a needle, then draw them through the fabric layers, and bring them up at the back of the quilt to tie off and snip.

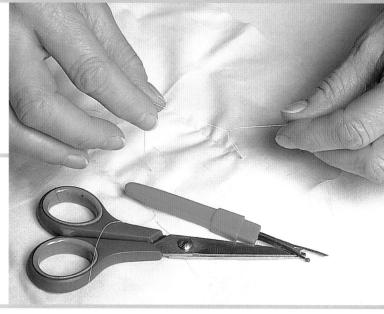

FREE MACHINE QUILTING

For free machine quilting, either drop the feed-dogs or cover them with a special plate, depending on your machine. Begin by taking a single stitch, turning the wheel manually, then bring the thread from the bobbin up to the top. This will ensure that it doesn't snarl up as you begin stitching.

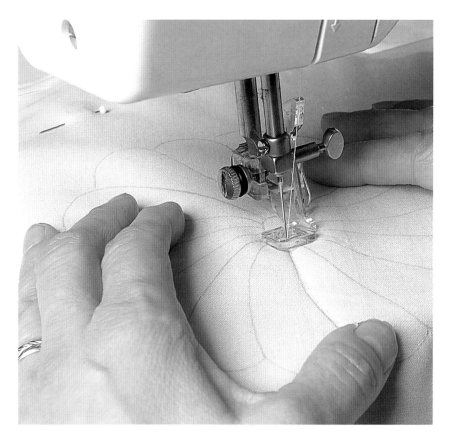

STEP 1
Fit a darning foot, or special quilting foot if provided with your machine. Set the needle length at 0 and lower the tension slightly. Make some samples as described for straight machine quilting. This is particularly important for free machine quilting, as learning to control the speed and movement of the work needs practice. Begin stitching, running the machine at a slightly slower rate than for ordinary sewing. As the feed-dogs are disconnected, you must move the quilt under the needle. Move it as evenly and steadily as possible – too fast and the stitches will be too small, too slow and the stitches will be too large. Start with some very simple quilting designs, which you can mark on the quilt top with pencil or other removable marker.

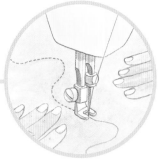

TIME-SAVER

The gardening gloves
mentioned on page 43 are
particularly useful for free
machine quilting, as you can
place your hands more firmly
on the quilt surface without
slipping, giving better control.

STEP 2 Practise 'meander' quilting,
moving the quilt under the needle to make
random patterns. When you feel confident
that you've got the idea and are happy with
your samples, begin on the quilt.

TIME-SAVER

Instead of marking the quilting design directly
onto the quilt, try drawing it on tracing paper,
pinning it onto the quilt top and stitching
through the paper. Tear paper away when
quilting is finished.

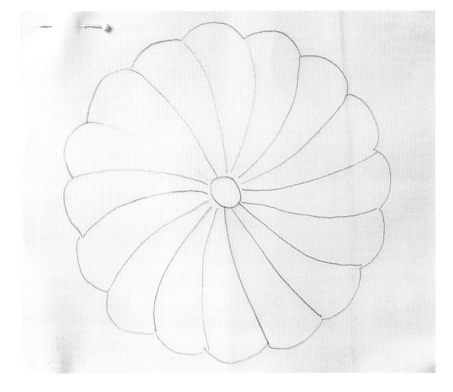

PROJECT 9:
MACHINE-QUILTED COT COVER

Finished size: 48 x 35 in. (122 x 89 cm)

This small, easily handled project is a mini-version of a traditional 'strippy' quilt. You can use it to practise your machine-quilting skills. It's quickly pieced and the quilting patterns, based on the authentic quilting designs that would be used on the full-sized version, have been adapted to suit the scale of the quilt. Many people prefer to use only natural materials in items intended for use by a baby, so for this project use cotton fabrics and, if necessary, pre-wash them to remove any stiffness or dressing. That way the quilt will be both practical and extremely soft for the baby to cuddle into. You can also get good-quality, washable cotton batting, but check with your supplier that it really is washable – otherwise it could bunch up in the quilt when you wash it (although as this quilt is well quilted all over, this is unlikely to happen).

WHAT YOU NEED

- 1.25 m (1¼ yards) each of two fabrics (small prints in white and blue are used in the quilt illustrated)
- 94 x 127 cm (37 x 50 in) backing fabric
- 94 x 127 cm (37 x 50 in) batting
- Quilting template – use template plastic if possible
- Walking foot for sewing machine (optional)
- Quilter's ruler

INSTRUCTIONS

STEP 1 First make the template.
Enlarge the shape given by 600 percent. Trace it and transfer the shape to template plastic or cardboard, taking care to include the notches. Cut out using scissors or a sharp craft knife.

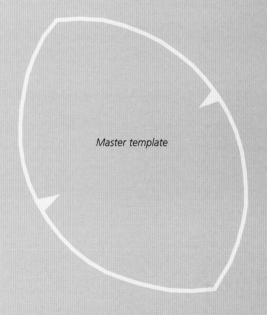

Master template

STEP 2
From the blue fabric: cut three pieces 19 x 123 cm (7½ x 48½ in). From white fabric: cut two pieces 19 x 123 cm (7½ x 48½ in).

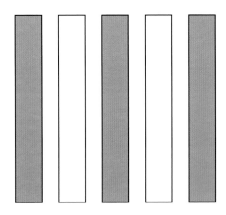

TIME-SAVER

At this stage, if you have some small pieces of fabric left over, it's worth making up a practice sample, using the same backing and batting as you're intending to use in the actual quilt. Practise on the sample, adjusting the stitch length and the tension until you're happy with them.

STEP 3
Join the strips along the long edges in this order: blue/white/blue/white/blue. Carefully press all the seams open.

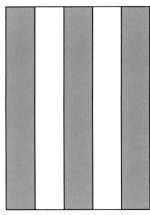

STEP 4
Lay out the quilt top on a firm, flat surface, preferably a table. Anchor it with masking tape at regular intervals around the edges.

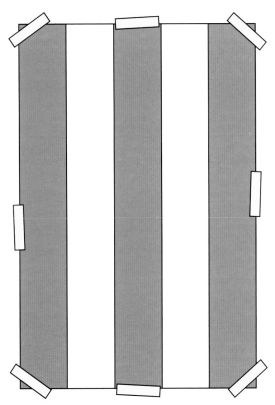

STEP 5
Use the templates to mark each blue strip, using either a soft (2B) pencil or a silver quilter's pencil. Mark a continuous row of ovals from top to bottom.

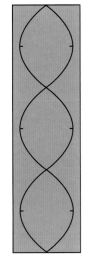

STEP 6
Go down the strip again, overlapping each shape by exactly half. Use the notches made on the template to line them up correctly.

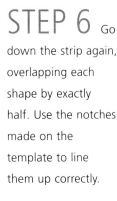

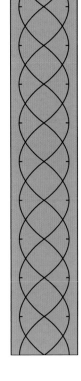

STEP 7
Use a quilter's ruler to mark the white strips in diagonal lines at 45 degrees, at 5 cm (2 in) intervals.

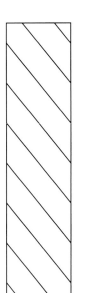

STEP 8 Crosshatch

the lines so as to form diamonds.

STEP 9 When

marking is complete, remove the masking tape and assemble the quilt for machine quilting. Pin and baste all over as described on page 34.

STEP 10 Prepare

for machine quilting by checking your machine as described on page 98. Attach a walking foot if you have one, and slightly reduce the tension.

STEP 11 Place

the first strip under the machine needle and support the rest of the quilt on a flat surface on your left. Stitch over the pattern in a continuous line from the top to the bottom. Start and end 1.25 cm (½ in) from the ends of the strips.

STEP 12 Start another line of

quilting from the top and stitch to the bottom. As the quilting progresses, feed the completed sections under the needle to your right and roll them up. Secure them with a clip or clips.

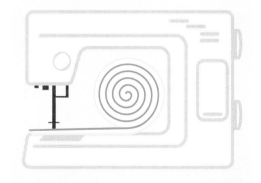

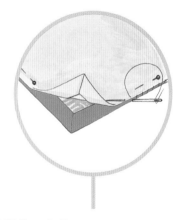

STEP 13 When all the quilting

is completed, trim back the backing and batting to the edge of the top. Finish the edges using the 'butted edge' method of finishing (see page 37).

TIME-SAVER

You can use a large bulldog clip to hold the part of the quilt you're not working on.

STEP 14 Most important of all,

to finish, make a label to sew on the back of the quilt, with the baby's name, your name and the date.

HAND APPLIQUÉ

Stitching shapes and motifs onto a contrasting background is one of the oldest ways known of decorating fabric. It probably began as a thrifty way of extending the life of textile items, whether clothes or household fabrics, by covering holes and worn areas with patches. Appliqué used in quiltmaking, particularly in blocks, also has a long history and has always been a popular technique among quilters. Appliqué can be worked by hand or by machine – both techniques are explained here.

You'll find many designs and motifs suitable for appliqué in magazines and books, or you can draw them for yourself. To begin with, choose motifs that are quite simple, without too many sharp angles or overlapping elements.

HAND APPLIQUÉ

WHAT YOU NEED
- Drawing paper
- Tracing paper
- Cardboard or template plastic
- Background fabric, such as good-quality muslin
- Fabrics for motifs
- Fine embroidery needle
- Ordinary sewing thread

The number of shapes that you can use in appliqué designs is unlimited and the shapes can be as simple or as complex as you like.

STEP 1 Draw the motif or design on paper and colour the shapes to identify the fabrics you'll use.

STEP 2 Trace each individual shape using tracing paper.

STEP 3 Transfer the shapes from the tracing paper to cardboard or template plastic and cut out. Prepare the background fabric by tracing over the drawing with a soft pencil or other marker so that you can see where to position the motifs.

STEP 4
Place the template on the right side of the fabric and draw around it using a No.2 pencil. For very dark fabrics, you may find it best to use a fine chalk pencil. Cut out the shape, leaving a generous 0.5 cm (¼ in) seam allowance all around it.

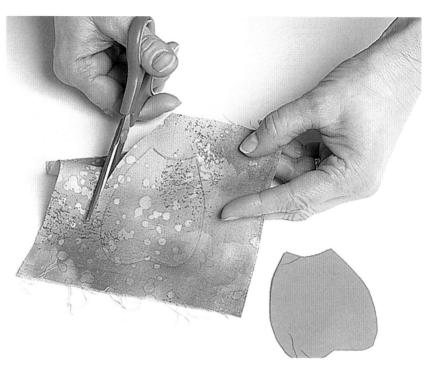

STEP 5
Prepare the shapes for sewing to the background. Firmly finger-press the seam allowance to the back of the shape, using the pencil line as a guide. Make sure the pencil line is not visible on the front of the shape. Alternatively, you can press the seam allowance turnings under with a hot iron to provide a crisp turning edge. Baste around the shape taking quite small stitches.

TIP

Notice that no turning is needed on a shape where it is overlapped by another one.

STEP 6
Prepare all the shapes in this way, and then pin them to the background. Make sure that the background is as smooth and flat as possible or your completed work won't lie flat.

TIME-SAVER
Get a really sharp turning on shapes by pressing the edges over the template first.

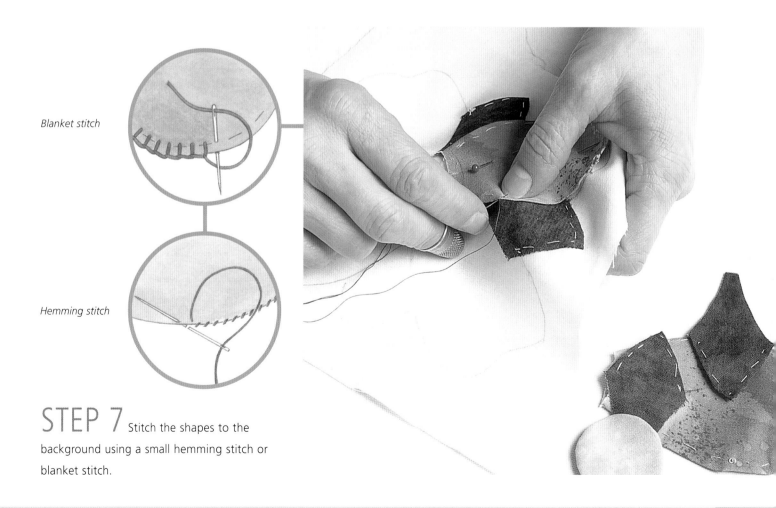

Blanket stitch

Hemming stitch

STEP 7
Stitch the shapes to the background using a small hemming stitch or blanket stitch.

PROJECT 10:
TULIP CUSHION

Finished size: 35 x 35 cm (14 x 14 in) plus frill

WHAT YOU NEED

- Cardboard
- 0.5 m (½ yard) fine quality cream muslin (for the background of the appliqué, the back of the cushion, and the frill)
- 41 x 41 cm (16 x 16 in) butter muslin
- 41 x 41 cm (16 x 16 in) thin batting
- Small pieces of two fabrics for the petals – a dark-and-light fabric combination is effective
- Small pieces of green fabric for the leaves
- 24 x 24 cm (9½ x 9½ in) piece of a darker green for the stems
- Sewing thread to match the fabric colours
- Cream-coloured quilting thread
- Quilting 'between' needle sizes 10 or 12
- Dressmaker's pins
- Cushion pad

The tulip has been a popular design motif ever since it was introduced to the West from Persia in the early seventeenth century. It has been used in just about every decorative arts and crafts medium, from tiles to embroidery to printed fabrics – and, of course, in quilts. This design is taken from an eighteenth-century quilt in which the appliqué blocks were made on a large scale. A single block will make an elegant cushion for your sitting room or bedroom, and once you've made one of these blocks, maybe you'll be inspired to go on and make some more for a quilt! Hand appliqué is an easy and satisfying technique that offers numerous possibilities for making quilt blocks and soft furnishings, or for decorating clothing. Hem stitches are used to anchor the shapes in this cushion, but you can just as easily use the blanket stitch shown on page 120. The background has been hand quilted with a diamond or crosshatching pattern. Notice that the stems are made from fabric strips cut on the bias so that they can be easily curved.

INSTRUCTIONS

STEP 1 Enlarge the design below by 35 times on to heavyweight paper. Go over the lines with a dark marker pen. Place the design on a flat surface and anchor all around with masking tape.

STEP 2 Place the background fabric evenly on top of the design and anchor that as well. Use a soft (2B) pencil or a quilter's silver pencil to outline the design on the background.

STEP 3
Identify the shapes to be used as A and B for the flowers and C for the leaves. You don't need to make templates for the stems. Follow the instructions on pages 104–107 to make templates, and to prepare the shapes to be appliquéd to the background.

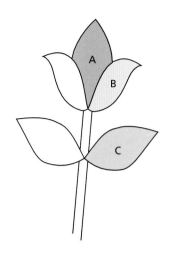

STEP 4
When all the flower and leaf shapes are ready, make the stems. Fold the dark green fabric in half diagonally and press well. Open out and cut through the pressed line. Cut strips 3 cm (1¼ in) wide on the diagonal.

Fold each strip in half lengthwise, wrong sides together, and stitch along the whole length, taking an exact 0.5 cm (¼ in) seam. Press the strip so that the joined edge is in the middle with the seam pressed to one side.

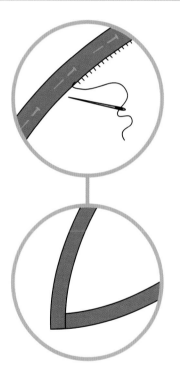

STEP 5
Pin strips over the stem lines on the background, using dressmaker's pins and easing the strips around the curves as you pin. Join the two ends at the bottom of the design by turning the end of one stem over the other. You can leave raw edges at the ends that will go under the flowers. Hem stitch the strips down.

STEP 6
Position a flower shape (A) over the design and pin. Position two flower shapes, one on each side of the first shape and pin again. Make sure that the patches cover the end of the stem. Using the hemming stitch shown on page 107, stitch first around shape A, to the points where it meets shapes B. Then stitch down both shapes B. Repeat this process for the other two flowers.

TIME-SAVER
Whenever you need to join strips to make a long length of fabric, overlap them and cut diagonally through both strips together. Place one on the other, right sides together, and stitch along the join.

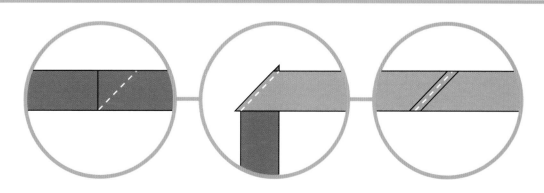

STEP 7
Position each of the leaves (shape C) and stitch them down in the same way.

STEP 8
When the appliqué is complete, anchor the background fabric to a flat surface and use the soft pencil and a ruler to mark diagonal lines 2.5 cm (1 in) apart across the surface in both directions.

STEP 9
Place the top on the batting and backing, and baste all over. Baste a temporary border around all four sides to enable you to quilt up to the edges (see page 55), and quilt along the marked lines.

TIME-SAVER
Make the hem stitches as invisible as possible by bringing the needle up exactly into the fold every time.

MAKING A FRILL

STEP 1
Cut a 13 x 213 cm (5 x 84 in) strip of muslin for the frill (you will need to join the strips). Fold it in half, and work a line of running stitches along the whole strip. Use a long machine stitch or sew by hand. Gather it up to fit the edge of the cushion top. Where the ends of the frill meet, overlap them and stitch together.

STEP 2
Baste the frill all around the front of the pillow form, with raw edges together.

STEP 3
Cut a muslin back for the cushion 36 x 36 cm (14¼ x 14¼ in). Join front to back, wrong sides together, anchoring the frill in the seam and leaving an opening to turn through.

STEP 4
Turn the whole cushion through the opening. Insert the pillow form and then close the opening by slipstitching.

Machine Appliqué

Machine appliqué provides a versatile way of creating many beautiful designs. It can be used to make all the traditional appliqué patterns found in quilt blocks, or you can use it to transfer to fabric original designs that you draw yourself. There are several machine appliqué techniques – the following are the most useful.

The first method, which uses fusible webbing, is the easiest. The webbing is on sheets of paper that you can draw on and cut to any size or shape you choose. The sticky side of the paper, which feels slightly rough, is pressed to the wrong side of the fabric using a hot iron. When the paper is peeled off, an adhesive layer is left on the fabric, which makes it possible to press it onto a background fabric.

Machine Appliqué using Fusible Webbing

What You Need
- Tracing paper
- Template plastic or cardboard
- Fusible webbing
- Background fabric
- Fabric for motifs
- Sewing machine
- Machine threads in different colours

STEP 1 Draw the pattern and make templates as for hand appliqué (see pages 104–107).

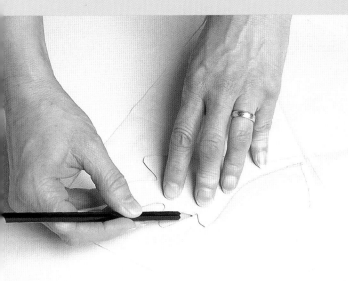

STEP 2 Mark the position of the shapes on the background fabric.

TIME-SAVER

If the shape to be applied is symmetrical, all you need to do is to fold and press creases in the background fabric.

STEP 3 Place the rough side of the fusible webbing paper onto the fabric selected for the motif and press with a hot iron.

STEP 4 Draw around the template using a soft pencil, then cut around the shape on the penciled line.

STEP 5
Peel off the paper to reveal a fine layer of adhesive on the fabric. Position the shape on the background and press firmly with a hot iron. You must wait until the fabrics have cooled before moving to the next step.

STEP 6
The two fabrics will be bonded together, but it's best to anchor them permanently by stitching round the edges of the shapes. Do this by working a zigzag machine stitch, using either contrasting or matching thread, depending on the effect you want to create. You can use an embroidery stitch for added interest. To finish, stitch all around the shape.

TIME-SAVER
You can also work machine appliqué by basting the edges of the shapes, as for hand appliqué (page 104), then stitching around the shapes using either a narrow hemming stitch or a fine zigzag stitch. Remove basting stitches when finished.

PROJECT 11:
FESTIVE STOCKING

Finished size: 33 x 20 cm (13 x 8 in)

WHAT YOU NEED

- 0.5 m (½ yard) of solid-coloured fabric in a bright colour – green or red, for example – for the stocking, lining and binding
- Medium interfacing (the iron-on type is best)
- Small pieces of a variety of Christmas fabrics
- Strip of lace 41 cm (16 in) long
- Small strip of satin ribbon for hanging loop
- Fusible webbing
- Machine-embroidery threads
- Cardboard or template plastic
- Tracing paper
- Heavyweight paper for pattern

Bring an original twist to your festive decorations with this bright and cheerful Santa stocking. Why not make several in different colourways to give to friends? You can even add names or initials to them if you like – children particularly love this personal touch. Although the sewing looks impressively complex, this method of appliqué is really easy to construct and needs a minimum of sewing. With such a vast array of special Christmas patchwork cotton fabrics on sale today your only problem will be which ones to choose! And since all the fabrics in this project are stabilized on fusible webbing, you can even include some more exotic fabrics, such as satin or silk to give that extra sparkle.

Master template

INSTRUCTIONS

STEP 1 Enlarge the stocking pattern given by 20 times. Trace it onto paper, and cut out the pattern.

STEP 2
Fold the solid stocking fabric in half and pin the pattern to it. Cut out all around. Mark the left and right sides of the stocking.

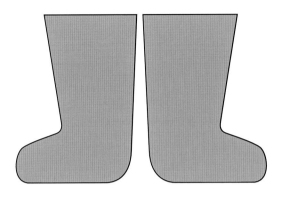

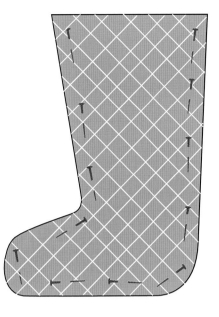

STEP 3
Cut out two pieces of interfacing in the same way. Pin a fabric shape to each interfacing. Pin and baste all around, or iron the shapes on if you are using iron-on interfacing.

STEP 4
Iron fusible webbing onto a selection of small pieces of Christmas fabrics (see page 112).

STEP 5
Make twelve triangles using an appropriate size of the triangle shape shown opposite. Arrange these as shown around the tops of the two sides of the stocking. Press carefully with a medium-hot iron.

0.5 cm (¼ in)   0.5 cm (¼ in)

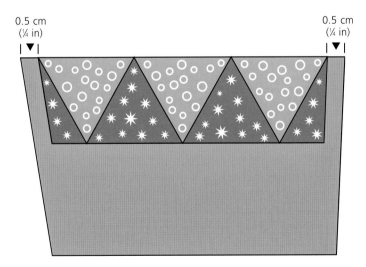

STEP 6
Draw around appropriate sizes of some of the other shapes shown opposite and cut them out. Arrange them in any way you like over the surface of the stocking. When you're happy with the arrangement, iron them in position.

STEP 7 Use decorative machine threads to outline the different shapes with zigzag stitches Add other decorations, such as ribbons if you like.

MAKING UP THE STOCKING

Now that you have made up the design of the outer part of the stocking, it is time to add the lining and assemble the pieces.

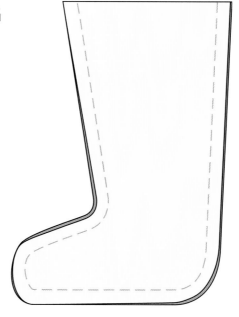

STEP 1 Use the pattern to cut out two stocking shapes from the lining fabric, and pin one to the inside of each side of the stocking. Pin the two sides of the stocking together, wrong sides together, and baste all around.

STEP 2 Cut 6 cm (2½ in) wide strips of binding fabric, cutting on the bias (see the instructions for stems on page 109, Step 4). Fold them in half and pin around the edge of the stocking, taking small tucks at the inner curves.

STEP 3 Stitch them all around, taking a 1.25 cm (½ in) seam. On the outer curves, snip through to the stitching line.

TIP

Grain describes the direction in which the threads of a fabric are woven. Fabric is made up of threads that run at right angles to each other on a loom. Bias strips are cut on the diagonal of a fabric and have quite a bit of stretch. They are therefore best used for curves.

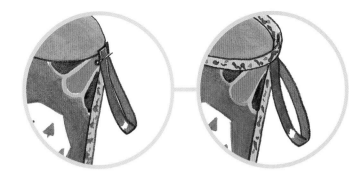

STEP 4 Turn the binding over the
seam and stitch neatly to the other side of the
stocking. Trim them even at both ends.

STEP 5 Make a hanging loop by doubling a piece
of ribbon and pinning it to the back seam. Stitch binding all
around the top of the stocking, anchoring the ends of the
ribbon loop. Turn and stitch to the inside.

STEP 6 Complete the stocking by
stitching a strip of lace all around the top,
below the triangles.

These stockings come out year after year in
my family, and it's fun to add names to them
so that you can think up suitable stocking-
fillers for everyone. But remember to reclaim
them after the festivities because they're very
collectable and you may end up, like me,
making several new ones each year!

EMBELLISHING QUILTS

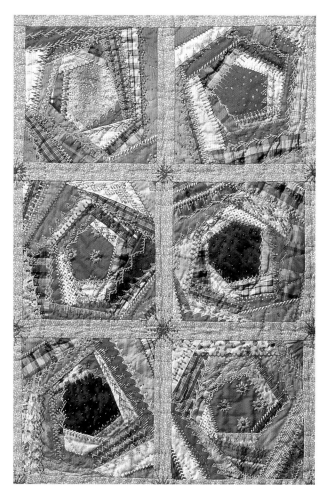

Attaching beads and sequins is easy and can add interesting texture and highlights to the quilt surface.

The fashion for embellishment was at its height in Victorian times, when Crazy patchwork was extravagantly decorated with embroidery, ribbons, lace, beads and sequins. The patchwork was made into table covers, throws, cushions, bags and many other items.

Today's quiltmakers are no less inventive, as a visit to any show or exhibition will quickly demonstrate. The boundaries between traditional craft and textile art are increasingly blurred and many people enjoy enhancing their quilts by using a whole repertoire of techniques, including those made familiar in the Crazy patchwork of yesteryear. Quilts nowadays are almost as likely to be seen on walls as on beds, so there is freedom to work with a wide range of fabrics and materials – even including some very unquilt-like media, like paper and plastic.

Here are a few techniques that you might like to try out for yourself. None of them are difficult and none requires materials that are difficult to acquire. However, this is one situation where making samples is a must – you need to learn what works for you and, if using the sewing machine, which threads, tensions and stitches are appropriate. This is your chance to be experimental and adventurous so try different materials and techniques before deciding which ones you want to use in a quilt.

EMBELLISHING QUILTS

WHAT YOU NEED

- Silks and perle cotton for hand embroidery
- Embroidery needles
- Embroidery threads for machine embroidery
- Special-purpose sewing machine needles for embroidery and for use with metallic thread
- Metallic threads
- Braids, lace, ribbons, beads, sequins

HAND EMBROIDERY AND TECHNIQUES

Embroidery is the art of decorating fabric with stitches to enrich or add to its beauty, and there are many embroidery stitches you can use to embellish your quilts. Practise the following stitches on single layers of fabric.

Feather Stitch

One of the most popular and effective stitches used on Crazy patchwork is the feather stitch. This is ideal for covering and decorating seams and is particularly effective if worked with perle cotton or brightly coloured silks. Follow the illustrations to see how to produce this simple stitch.

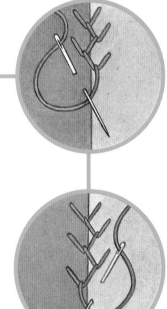

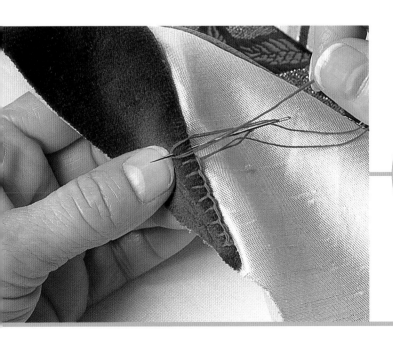

Blanket Stitch

The blanket stitch is often used to cover seams and to stitch appliqué motifs to background fabric. It is simple and easy to work and may be varied easily in sizing and spacing for various decorative effects.

Chain stitch

The chain stitch is often used to embellish seams and to embroider stems and motifs. It forms bold, fluid lines that are easily curved to suit sinuous natural forms.

Beads, sequins and lace

Attaching beads and sequins is easy and can add interesting texture and highlights to the quilt surface. Use the embroidery stitches both to cover seams and to decorate patches.

Use ribbons, laces and braids in the same way.

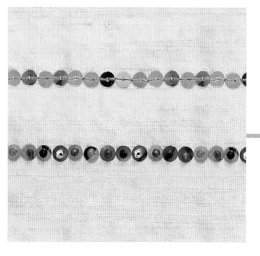

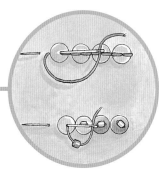

Couching

Couching involves laying threads along the line of a design and anchoring it by stitching over it with contrasting coloured threads. You can use quite thick threads which will make the design stand out.

'Broderie Perse'

'Broderie perse' is one of the earliest embroidery techniques, in which motifs and designs are cut from printed fabrics and applied to the surface of the quilt. Carefully cut out the motif and pin in position. Anchor it by sewing around it with blanket stitch or by machine-sewn zigzag stitch.

TIME-SAVER

Use the fusible webbing method described on pages 111–113 for applying the motifs before stitching around them.

Machine Embroidery and Techniques

Most of the techniques described on pages 119–121 can be worked on the sewing machine. It's important to check your machine first, as success with these techniques depends on a well-maintained and efficiently operating machine, along with a thorough understanding of what it will and won't do. Remove any build-up of lint around the bobbin and carry out any necessary oiling and maintenance.

Be sure to use the right needles and threads for the job you're doing. For example, when using metallic threads it's essential to use one of the special needles that have a slightly larger eye than average. This is to allow the thread to run smoothly through the needle without being frayed. There are also special needles for machine embroidery threads.

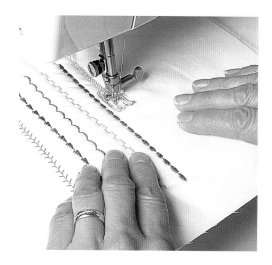

Instructions

Cut several squares of fine muslin 25 x 25 cm (10 x 10 in) square. Pin them to 25 cm (10 in) squares of backing fabric and batting. Use these to practise the various techniques.

In addition to the plain zigzag stitches on appliqué shapes described in Machine Appliqué (see page 113), try using some of the more elaborate embroidery stitches on your machine.

Of course, you will be limited by the number and variety of embroidery stitches available on your particular sewing machine, but most modern machines have a useful selection. Try using coloured machine embroidery threads. Metallic threads also produce striking effects.

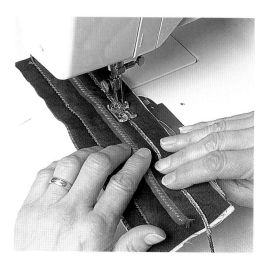

Fabric Manipulation

This involves creating texture by such means as ruching, pleats and tucks.

Ribbons can be ruched to produce an attractive ruffled effect. Work a line of straight running stitch through the centre of the ribbon and draw up to the length required.

Tucks and pleats add texture. Fold and pin the fabric before stitching.

These are just a few of the many techniques that can be used to embellish and enhance your quilts. To find out more about this fascinating aspect of quilting, look for one of the many books about Crazy quilts, both modern and traditional.

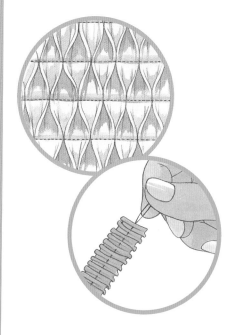

DECORATIVE WALL-PANEL

Finished size: 132 x 132 cm (52 x 52 in)

This is your chance to really branch out and experiment with some of the many different techniques now used in quiltmaking. The panel comprises sixteen 20 cm (8 in) blocks in the Crazy Log Cabin patchwork style, using a variety of fabrics of varying texture and sheen. The blocks are joined with narrow sashing strips, with bead embroidery where they meet. Each block can be heavily embellished with embroidery, couching or whatever techniques you choose. The palette of predominantly pinks and reds in the quilt shown here creates a wonderfully rich effect, but other colour schemes can be just as effective. Home-dyed and painted fabrics and embellishments of every sort are seen on many quilts exhibited in shows – these are often described as 'textile art' rather than as quilts. So, if you want to expand your horizons, this is the project for you. All the techniques described here are covered in Embellishing Quilts (pages 118–122).

WHAT YOU NEED

- Sixteen 23 x 23 cm (9 x 9 in) muslin foundation squares
- Selection of scraps of fabrics of your choice – try to include some shiny satins and silks
- 0.5 m (½ yard) of fabric for sashings and binding
- 0.5 m (½ yard) of fabric for the border
- Threads for hand and machine embroidery in a variety of colours
- Beads, sequins, ribbons, lace and braids
- Piece of batting 132 x 132 cm (52 x 52 in)
- Piece of backing fabric 132 x 132 cm (52 x 52 in)

INSTRUCTIONS

Note: The Crazy Log Cabin technique is based on the traditional method of making Log Cabin blocks, except that the logs are cut and placed randomly around the centre patch, which itself need not necessarily be square. This version has a five-sided patch in the centre.

STEP 1 Place a
piece of fabric of any shape on the foundation square and pin in place. It doesn't have to be exactly in the middle.

STEP 2 Cut a
strip of another fabric and place it right sides together along one edge of the first patch. Stitch it down, flip it open and press lightly.

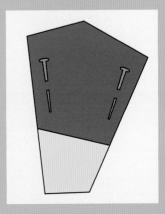

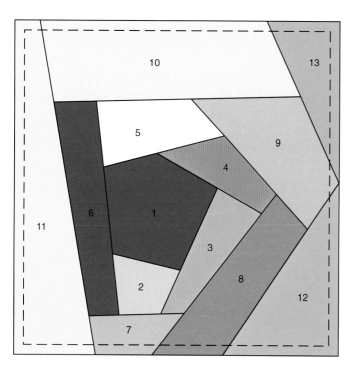

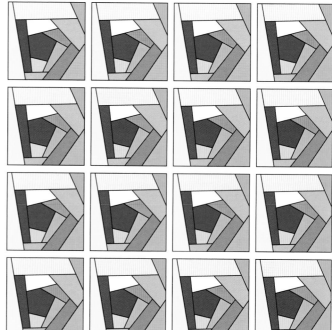

STEP 3
Add another strip around the centre patch in the same way. Continue like this, adding strips of different widths until the foundation is completely covered. The final round of strips should extend over the edge of the foundation. Turn to the back of the block and trim each block to make an 21 cm (8½ in) square. Baste all around the edges to secure the pieced block to the foundation.

STEP 4
Make sixteen blocks like this. Cut sashing strips 7.5 cm (3 in) wide and join the blocks in rows with the strips between them (see pages 41–42).

STEP 5
Add a 10 cm (4 in) border all around (see pages 31–32).

STEP 6 Mount the pieced panel on batting and backing, pinning and basting all over. Stitch 'in the ditch' (see page 43) through all the seams between the blocks and the sashings.

STEP 7 To embellish the blocks, first machine embroider over some of the seams with a variety of the stitches shown in Embellishing Quilts (pages 119–121). Notice that you'll be combining quilting and embellishment as you sew through all three layers.

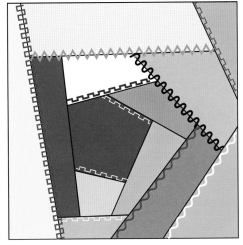

STEP 8 Add further details with hand-embroidery stitches using bright threads. Apply couching over some of the seams using contrasting threads and applied ribbons, braid, sequins and beads. Treat each pieced block separately, and try to make each one as bright and as striking as possible.

STEP 9 At points where sashings meet, embroider a 'spider's web' pattern with bright threads and beads.

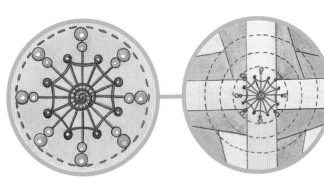

STEP 10 When all the embellishment is complete, trim the backing and batting even with the top of the panel, and bind all round (see page 34).

GLOSSARY

Appliqué The technique of applying one piece of fabric to the surface of another fabric, either by hand or by machine.

Backing (Also batting) Bottom layer or lining of quilt.

Backstitch A stitch taken backwards from the direction of sewing to reinforce the beginning or end of a seam.

Baste (Also tack) To work large running stitches as a temporary anchor before final stitching.

Batting (Also wadding) The filling layer placed between the quilt top and backing.

Bias The diagonal direction of a woven fabric.

Binding The edging of a quilt which covers and holds all raw edges. Bindings may be plain or decorative.

Block A square of patchwork that is a complete design in itself. Blocks are sewn together to make a quilt.

Border The piece or pieces of fabric that frame the outside of the quilt top.

Broderie perse Technique of cutting out printed motifs and applying them to a background fabric.

English Patchwork A patchwork technique in which the fabric patches are basted over paper templates. The templates are only removed when the pieces have been sewn to each other and the entire quilt top is complete.

Fat quarter A piece of fabric measuring approximately 46 x 46 cm (18 x 18 in).

Finger press To make a crease by pressing fabric between the fingers.

Free machine quilting Machine quilting with the sewing machine feed-dogs disengaged.

Marking Tracing or drawing quilting lines using chalk, quilter's pencils or other markers.

Mitre To join two pieces of fabric so that the ends meet at a right angle with a diagonal seam.

Monofilament Single-filament synthetic thread which is clear and therefore also called 'invisible thread.'. Typically used for quilting 'in the ditch'.

Muslin Plain, unbleached cotton cloth.

On point Mounting a square block at an angle in a quilt top so that it appears as a diamond.

Overcast (Also oversew) Working stitches loosely over fabric edges to join them or prevent them from fraying.

Patchwork Joining one or more fabric shapes together to make a pattern.

Quilting The process of securing all three layers of quilt (quilt top, batting and backing) together with a decorative pattern of small running stitches.

Quilt top The completed patchwork design used as the right side or face of a quilt. It is the top layer of a quilt.

Rotary cutter A circular blade used for cutting several layers of fabric simultaneously.

Running stitch A straight stitch, used for most hand quilting.

Sashing Strips placed between blocks in a quilt.

Scrap quilt A quilt made up of a mixture of fabrics, usually remnants from other projects.

Seam allowance The area of fabric between the stitching line and the cut edge. The seam allowance allows room for handing and adjusting size.

Stitching 'in the ditch' Quilting worked directly over a seam.

Template Pattern cut in cardboard, plastic or other firm material for marking shapes on fabric.

Walking foot Quilt-making attachment for the sewing machine which feeds top and bottom layers evenly under the needle. Also known as an 'even-feed foot'.

Whipstitch A stitch that holds together two finished edges. The needle is inserted at right angles to the edge through both fabrics.

Zigzag A basic machine sewing back-and-forth stitch; it has width as well as length.

INDEX

Author's Acknowledgements

Grateful thanks to my quilting friends, Debbie Woolley and
Carolyn Madden, for making some of the project quilts:

Ribbon Quilt by Carolyn Madden
Barn Raising Log Cabin Quilt and Machine-Quilted
Crib Cover by Debbie Woolley
Amish-style Wall Quilt by Sandie Lush

Thanks to Lorraine Mitchell and Debbie Woolley for
lending quilts for photography.

Special thanks to Maggie Barber for lending her quilt 'Tutti
Fruit' for photography and inspiration.